Ancient Peoples and Places

THE CANAANITES

General Editor

DR GLYN DANIEL

ABOUT THE AUTHOR

John Gray was educated at Kelso High School and took his M.A., B.D., and Ph.D. degrees at Edinburgh University. He was C. B. Black Scholar in Hellenistic Greek, 1936–1939, and also Blackie Travelling Fellow of Edinburgh University in the Near East, 1936–1937; he was introduced to field archaeology by the late J. L. Starkey at Tell ed-Duweir. From 1939 to 1941 he served as Chaplain to the Palestine Police in the Northern Area in Palestine and returned to be Minister of the Church of Scotland, Kilmory, Isle of Arran from 1942–1947. In 1947 he became Assistant Lecturer and subsequently Lecturer in Semitic Languages and Literature in the University of Manchester. From 1952 he was Lecturer in Hebrew and Biblical Criticism at the University of Aberdeen where he was appointed to the Professorship of Hebrew and Semitic Languages in 1962.

Professor Gray is the author of several books on aspects of Canaan and its literature and commentaries on the Old Testament.

Ancient Peoples and Places

THE CANAANITES

John Gray

61 PHOTOGRAPHS
54 LINE DRAWINGS
3 MAPS

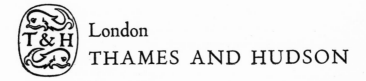

T&H
London
THAMES AND HUDSON

THIS IS VOLUME THIRTY-EIGHT IN THE SERIES
Ancient Peoples and Places
GENERAL EDITOR: DR GLYN DANIEL

PRINTED IN GREAT BRITAIN BY
HAZELL WATSON AND VINEY LTD, AYLESBURY, BUCKS
NOT TO BE IMPORTED FOR SALE INTO THE U.S.A.

CONTENTS

ILLUSTRATIONS

Foreword

THE CENTRAL SITUATION of Syria and Palestine in the ancient Near East singles out their inhabitants, the Canaanites, as an obvious subject in this series *Ancient Peoples and Places,* and this study, limited to the second millennium BC, the formative period of Canaanite culture, is the natural introduction to Dr D. B. Harden's study on *The Phoenicians* in the same series.

Canaan as revealed by field archaeology in Palestine and by the political correspondence of its chiefs in the Amarna Tablets was the subject of a substantial work by the doyen of Palestinian archaeology, the late R. P. L. H. Vincent, O.P. in 1907. Since then evidence from Canaan has multiplied many fold by the excavation of many more important sites in Syria and Palestine than had been then excavated, and by much improved methods. The spectacular discoveries from royal tombs at Byblos, from temples and palaces at Megiddo and Bethshan, and above all from the Baal temple, the palace, and town of Ras Shamra, and less spectacular, but still important, material from many other sites have provided a wealth of important data for comparative study, while the recovery beyond all expectation of a substantial amount of the literature of Canaan and administrative documents from Ras Shamra has made a synthesis of both kinds of evidence imperative. With the new material the question of the originality of Canaanite art may be examined.

The value of the Canaanite literature and administrative texts from Ras Shamra on the eve of the Hebrew settlement is, we believe, much greater than is generally realized, too great indeed to be the subject of broad generalizations, which characterize sections devoted to the subject in many text-books of Old

Testament study. Since both too much and too little has been claimed for these discoveries, a detailed study is highly desirable, and that conviction has stimulated our own specialized studies in this field. We trust that within the strict limitations of the present work a fair impression is conveyed of the scope and significance of this revolutionary new material, and hope that before exception is taken to our broadly stated conclusions our detailed studies on the subject, especially in the *Legacy of Canaan* (2nd ed., 1964), may be fairly considered.

Throughout the present work we have endeavoured to simplify readings by omitting accents and diacritic notations from transliterations of Semitic words. The exception is the sibilant *s*, i.e. *š*, to be read *sh*.

Here we would take the opportunity to pay tribute to the pioneer work of M. Charles Virolleaud, *editor princeps* in both senses of the term, and of the late M. René Dussaud. If we have not accepted all their conclusions we should certainly have achieved much less without the stimulus of their original genius and lively vision. The more restrained work of Professor C. H. Gordon, who provided a corpus of the texts in transliteration, in which they were readily accessible, and an excellent working grammar, also merits our respect, as do also the more recent translations and philological notes of Professor G. R. Driver (*Canaanite Myths and Legends*, 1956) and the late Professor J. Aistleitner (*Die mythologischen und kultischen Texte aus Ras Schamra*, 1959; *Wörterbuch der ugaritischen Sprache*, 1963). We owe the last book to Professor O. Eissfeldt, Halle (Saale), who edited the work after the death of Professor Aistleitner in 1960, and who generously sent us the gift of the book. Professor Eissfeldt also deserves our gratitude for his excellent constructive and critical work on the recently discovered administrative texts from the palace of Ras Shamra and for a series of studies on the religion of Canaan.

In the preparation of the present work I have been supported by the help and encouragement of many friends. The distinguished excavator of Ras Shamra, Professor C. F. A. Schaeffer, who has put us all so much in his debt not only by his methodical and felicitous field work but by his lucid and regular reports and by his magisterial *Stratigraphie Comparée et Asie Occidentale Chronologie d'*, has shown me many personal kindnesses, which I now again acknowledge, thanking him particularly for his cordial consent to publish plates and figures of Ras Shamra material, which is acknowledged in detail in the citation of these. With those whose generous help in obtaining illustrations I acknowledge in another place I should like particularly to thank those whom I met personally while engaged in research in Palestine, Syria, and the Lebanon: R. P. Roland de Vaux, O. P. of the French School of Archaeology and Dr Yussuf Sa'ad, the Director of the Palestine Archaeological Museum in Jerusalem, M. l'Emir Maurice Chehab, the Director of the National Museum in Beirut and his assistant M. Roger Sa'id, and Mr Faisal Seirafi, the Director of Antiquities and Museums in North Syria and Aleppo, to whose generosity I owe many of my illustrations, and whose cordial welcome and co-operation expedited my local researches and made my visit among them not only profitable but most pleasant.

In the preparation of the manuscript I am most grateful to my able young assistant the Reverend William Johnstone, Lecturer in the Department of Hebrew and Semitic Languages in the University of Aberdeen, who, with characteristic acumen and thoroughness, read it and prepared the index. Mr Johnstone, on his return from his work at Ras Shamra with Professor Schaeffer, undertook the revision of proofs together with my wife, and to both I am deeply indebted.

I gratefully acknowledge the help of Mr H. A. Shelley in preparing the maps, and of Mr M. L. Rowe of Cambridge and Mr M. Spink of Thames & Hudson in preparing such line drawings as I have acknowledged elsewhere in detail. In the rest of the figures and plans I have had the benefit of the professional skill of my friend Mr James L. Somerville, A.R.I.B.A. of Aberdeen. Mr Somerville's patient work, his genuine interest in the wider scope of my work, and his helpful criticism in our frequent discussions have proved invaluable.

Finally my thanks are due to Dr Glyn Daniel and the editorial staff of Thames & Hudson for their patient forbearance in the delays occasioned by illustrations and for their ever helpful guidance in the many details involved in the preparation of this work. J. G.

CHAPTER I

Introduction

THE CANAANITES are generally known through the Old Testament as the major element in the population of Palestine dispossessed by Israel in her occupation of the 'land flowing with milk and honey'. With great indignation and broad generalization 'the abominations of the Canaanites' are stigmatized by Hebrew prophets, reformers, and editors of the Old Testament. They roundly condemn their people for going 'a-whoring after the Baalim' and Ashtaroth, the local manifestations of the deities of the Canaanite fertility-cult, which they caricature by referring to one element in it, sexual licence, as a rite of imitative magic to induce the liberality of Providence in nature. Our present project is to use material and documentary data of the Canaanites themselves, so liberally furnished by modern archaeology, to particularize and present a more objective picture of the Canaanites and their way of life.

'Canaan' derives from *kinahna*, by which the Semites of Mesopotamia in the second millennium denoted the Syrian coast from the Gulf of Alexandretta to Carmel Head; from it they obtained the much-prized purple dye (*kinahhu*), produced from the shell-fish native to these shores. This narrower and more specific application of the name Canaan is known also in the Old Testament, e.g. Josh. 13.4 (the neighbourhood of Sidon), Isa. 23.11 (Tyre), and possibly Judg. 5.19 ('kings of Canaan' in alliance with Sisera in the west of the great central plain of Palestine near Megiddo). The last reference extends the term to include the inhabitants of the large settlements of that plain and of Upper Galilee (e.g. Hazor), which maintained contact with the cities of the Syrian coast (Phoenicia or Canaan proper) and shared their culture and religion, as archaeology has so abundantly demonstrated. A further extension of the terms is made in Num. 13.29, which locates the Canaanites by the seashore and the Jordan. Such a centre of culture and commerce was Hazor in the plain of the upper Jordan commanding the fords south of Lake Huleh on the road to Damascus and the road to the north over the watershed between the Jordan and the Litani (Leontes) to the Phoenician coast. The King of Hazor is called 'the King of Canaan' in Judg. 4.2, 23–24. The term Canaan has a similar extension in the correspondence of the Egyptian government with chiefs and Egyptian officers in Syria and Palestine in the Tell el-Amarna Tablets (*c.* 1411–1358). The term then was loosely applied by the Hebrews to their predecessors in Palestine, though the enumeration of Canaanites along with Amorites, Hittites, Hivites, Perizzites, Girgashites, and Jebusites indicates an awareness of the extraordinary ethnic diversity in the land.

We are more specifically informed on this ethnic situation in the nomenclature in the Amarna Tablets; these leave no doubt that 'Canaan' and 'Canaanites', while occasionally used in the Old Testament to denote the whole of Palestine and its pre-Israelite inhabitants, denote a culture rather than a distinct ethnic group. Insofar as there is any ethnic significance in the term this is secondary, and denotes the Semites, who were the largest element in the population and who stamped their ethos on the culture and language. Actually as an ethnic term denoting the Semitic substratum of the population of Syria and Palestine in the second millennium 'Amorite' is more appropriate than 'Canaanite'. The comparative unity of culture in Syria and Palestine, which the common term 'Canaan' implies, is demonstrated by the substantial agreement between the Old Testament references to Canaanite culture, by material remains from various archaeological sites in the area, and by the abundant documentary evidence from Ras Shamra.

Palestine and Syria lacked the natural advantage of a great river like the Euphrates and Tigris, or the Nile, which invited co-operation in irrigation and facilitated the pooling of technical skill and resources and so brought Mesopotamia and Egypt to the forefront in culture and political development. The western escarpment of Syria and Palestine, however, was watered by winter rain from the clouds borne by the prevailing wind from the sea to the inland deserts and by heavy dew from spring to late summer, but the eastern escarpment in Palestine was in the rain-shadow. Such conditions, though not unfavourable, promoted only limited communal development, producing independent communities concentrated in necessarily limited numbers about local springs and cultivable tracts, and often isolated by the diversified nature of the land. Living from season to season, occasionally at subsistence level, under constant threat of periodic drought, locusts from the desert, or nomadic incursion, these communities developed toughness and resilience, but politically they developed little. Thus the phenomenon of a territorial state embracing the whole of the area was exceptional and not of permanent duration. Culturally too the inhabitants of this region were limited, being content to assimilate elements from the cultures of Egypt and Mesopotamia, and of Crete and Mycenae.

The Canaanites were essentially middlemen in traffic, in war and peace, diplomacy, trade, and culture between Mesopotamia and Egypt. This fact is very well illustrated by *Fig. 1* material remains from the various archaeological stations, particularly from Ras Shamra, ancient Ugarit, on the north Syrian coast, where Egyptian political influence and Mesopotamian commercial interests are well attested when the city was at its apogee in the Late Bronze Age (*c.* 1600–1200). And as middlemen the Canaanites were thus enabled by virtue of their unique location to make their greatest contribution to human progress, the alphabet.

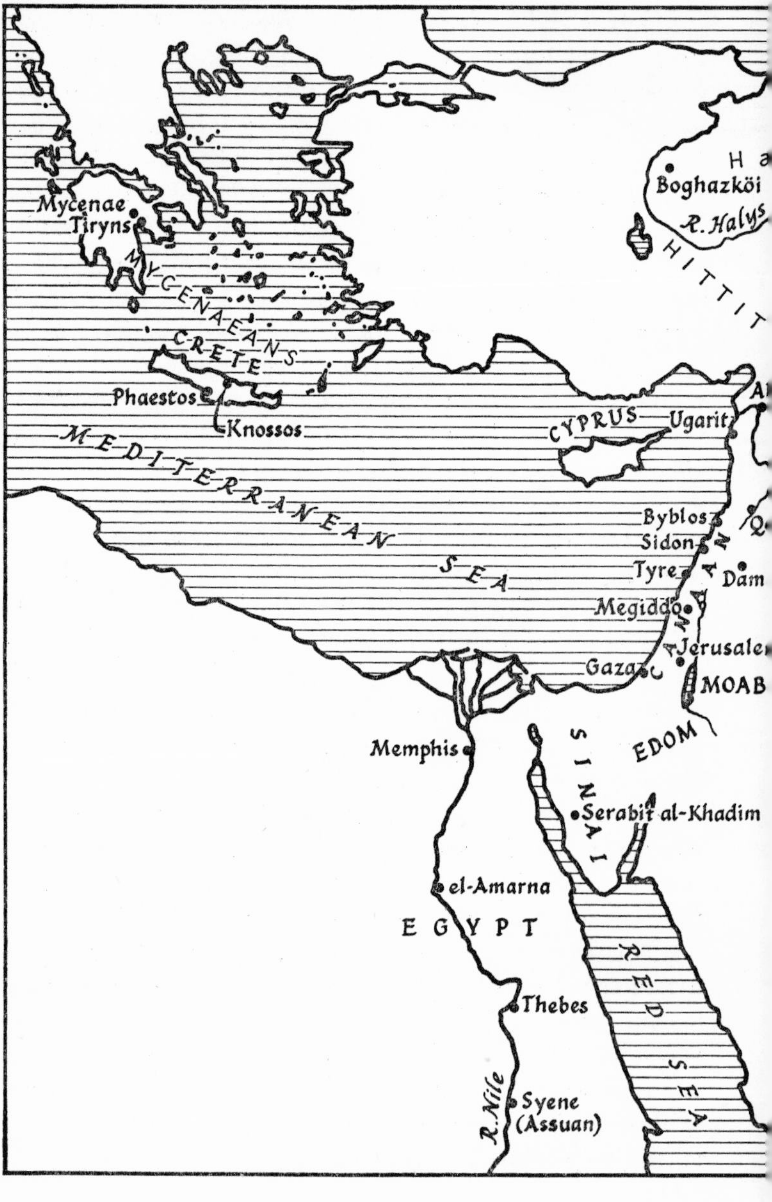

Fig. 1. The Near East in the second millennium B.C.

CASPIAN SEA
URARTU
MITANNI
rchemish
Arslan Tash
Nineveh (Kouyunjik)
MORITES
or
Mari
o-ARAMEANS
R. Tigris
Babylon
Susa
ELAM
R. Euphrates
ARABIA
PERSIAN GULF
0
100
200
300
400
500
Scale of Miles

The excellent synthesis of archaeological data by the great Dominican archaeologist, the late R. P. L. H. Vincent, *Canaan d'après l'Exploration Récente* (1900), was of necessity a *Fig. 2* pioneer work, being strictly confined to Palestinian sites so far excavated. Some of these, such as Tell ez-Zakariyeh, Tell Judeideh, Tell es-Sandahannah, and Tell es-Safi in the western foothills of Judah, were limited enterprises of no great significance for our study. One site in this area, Tell el-Hesy (possibly Eglon) at the edge of the coastal plain some 15 miles from Gaza, is significant as the first stratified mound where the typological dating of Sir Flinders Petrie was employed by that illustrious pioneer and by F. J. Bliss (1891–93). Jerusalem, also excavated at this time (1894–97), was disappointing, but the work at Tell Taʿanek, Gezer, and Megiddo was much more extensive and fruitful, and it was mainly from the data from those sites that Père Vincent reconstructed his Canaan. After the Great War the scientific technique of archaeology was developed to a very high degree, and, following the principles of typological dating of which Petrie and Vincent were notable exponents, there is now general agreement in the dating of strata and in the duration and succession of cultural phases. For the horizon has expanded far beyond the scope of Père Vincent's book. Our study now not only includes much more extensive data and involves a reassessment of earlier work in Palestine, but it is also vastly enriched by the much more extensive work at Megiddo, Tell el-ʿAjjul, Tell Jemmeh, and Tell el-Farʿa in *Figs. 2, 3* the Wadi Ghazzeh, Tell Beit Mirsim (probably ancient Qiryath Sepher also called Debir), Tell ed-Duweir (probably ancient Lachish) in the south-western foothills of Judah, Bethel, Bethshan, Jericho, Shechem, Tell el-Farʿa by Nablus, Tell Qasileh by Jaffa, Tell Abu Hawam by Haifa, and most recently Hazor in Palestine and Byblos and Ras Shamra on the Syrian coast and Qatna, Hama, and Atchana (ancient Alalakh) in the Orontes Valley. Besides these major excava-

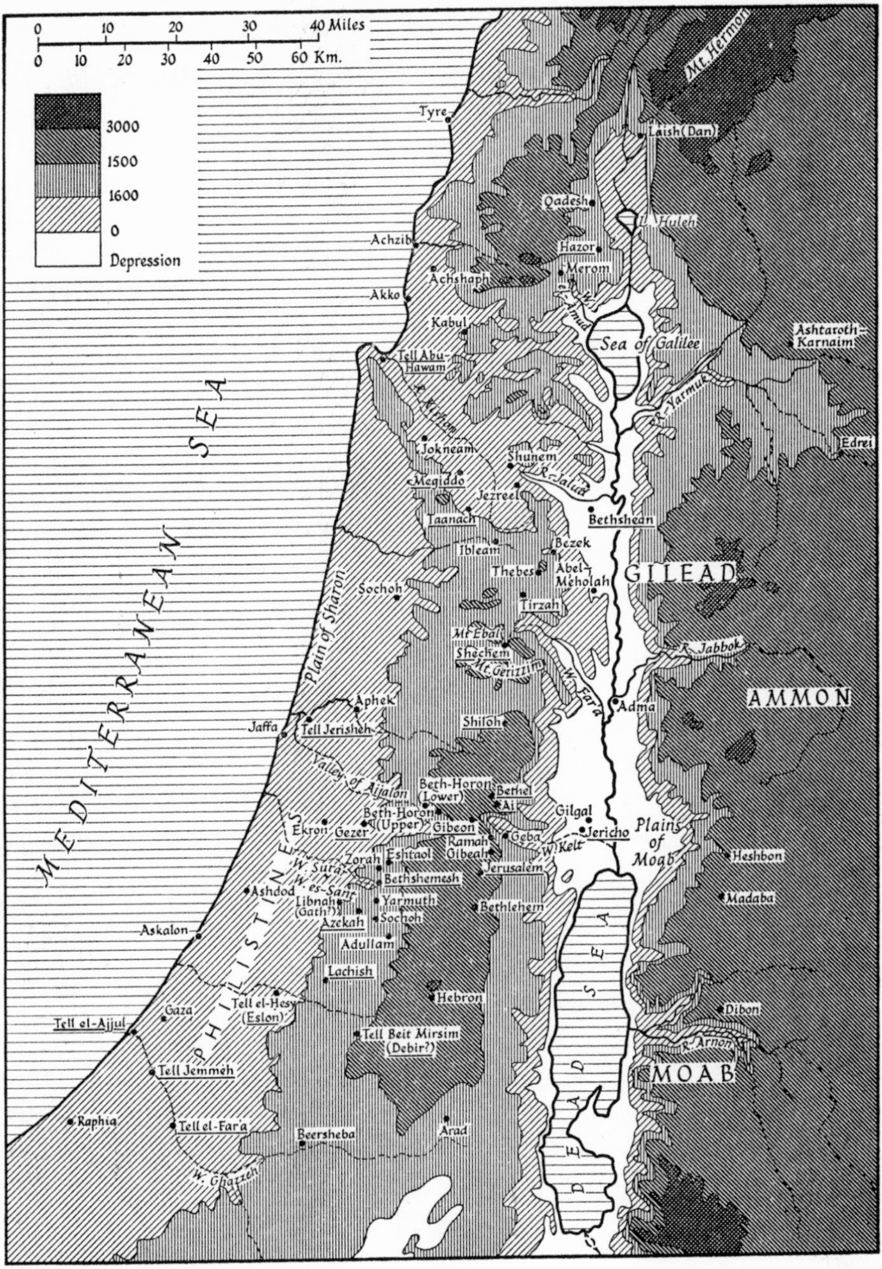

Fig. 2. Palestine in the Bronze Age

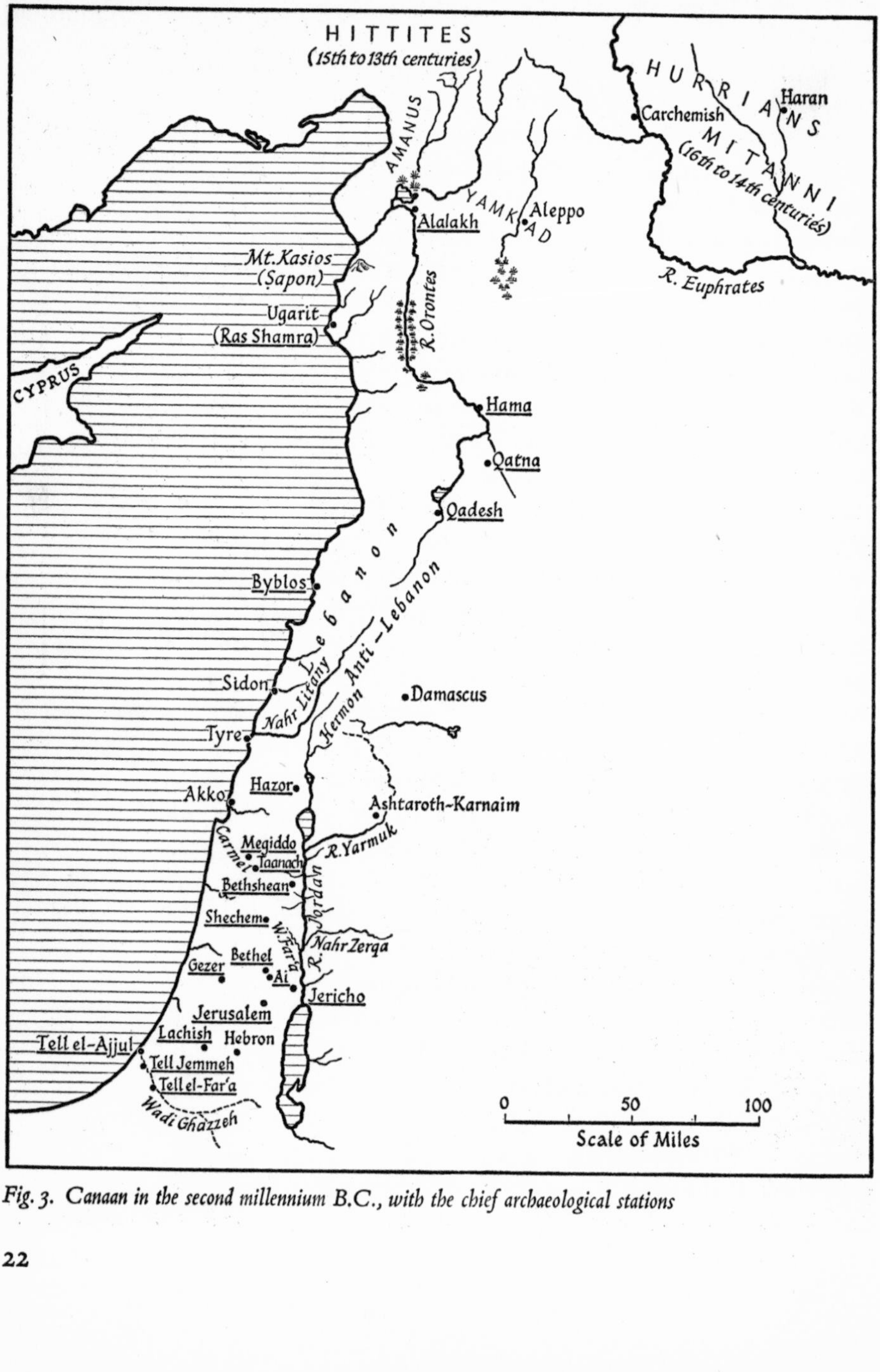

Fig. 3. Canaan in the second millennium B.C., with the chief archaeological stations

tions there were also many small tomb clearances and soundings. The development of life in the Near East from the earliest ages has been richly illustrated from these and other excavations in the area, such as Mari on the mid-Euphrates, but we shall of set purpose limit our study to the history and culture of Canaan in the second millennium, by which Israel was confronted in her settlement and which was formative in Phoenician culture in the last pre-Christian millennium. From this extended archaeological field new factors have emerged which have necessitated a shifting of the centre of gravity in such a survey since Père Vincent's study of Canaan. Palestine, which is central in his study, proves to be provincial in comparison to the great cities of the Syrian coast.

Apart from the Egyptian Amarna Tablets, which are primarily political, Père Vincent relied on material evidence, which was in the nature of the case fragmentary. While this indicated the types of fortifications, dwellings, and public buildings, such as temples, and particularly by means of pottery types distinguished the main cultural phases in the history of the land and the source of foreign influences, there was necessarily a large subjective element in such a reconstruction as far as concerned the internal life and thought of the people. Now this field of conjecture is happily very much reduced. The hypotheses of Père Vincent have been tested and modified or substantiated not only by added material data from many more archaeological stations now understood much more fully in the whole context of the ancient Near East, but this matter has itself been supplemented by a flood of documentary evidence from the second millennium. The linear alphabetic inscriptions from Sinai and Lachish, the inscriptions of Shaphat-Baal and Ahiram from Byblos, and the calendar from Gezer of the tenth century, short as these are, would have been notable acquisitions. They are dwarfed, however, by the mass of inscribed tablets from Ras Shamra in

Akkadian syllabic and Canaanite alphabetic cuneiform, which illustrate the politics, society, religion, and literature of Canaan in the Late Bronze Age, especially in the fourteenth and thirteenth centuries. Supplemented by Akkadian tablets from Atchana these greatly amplify the picture of the political situation in north Syria in the Amarna Tablets and make explicit various items of social and religious significance which, being incidental to the main purport of the Amarna Tablets, were formerly obscure. From beyond Canaan itself, light on the political and cultural contacts of the land with Mesopotamia in the age of Hammurabi of Babylon (*fl. c.* 1700) is shed by cuneiform texts from the chancellery of the Amorite city of Mari, and from Egypt the inscriptions already known in the time of Père Vincent have been supplemented by fresh discoveries, notably by magical texts from the nineteenth century, which relate to the settlement of Amorite tribes in the strategic centres of south Syria and Palestine, which we know as Canaanite centres in the second millennium.

A clear picture of Canaanite civilization from its inception and formative period at the end of the third millennium to its apogee in the fourteenth–thirteenth centuries could almost be reconstructed on this epigraphic evidence alone, and indeed, for the last phase, on the evidence of the Ras Shamra texts alone, so tremendously significant are they. These texts, however, full and extensive though they are beyond the most sanguine hopes of scholars of a generation ago, are still fragmentary, hence nothing in the whole range of archaeology in Syria and Palestine and the immediate neighbourhood may be neglected if we would fill out the picture of Canaan in the Middle and Late Bronze Ages (*c.* 2000–1200) in its general cultural unity with variations imposed by local ecology.

CHAPTER II

Habitat and History

CANAAN WAS A NEXUS of communications from various directions. The stepping-stone between Egypt, Mesopotamia, and Anatolia, it was also the bridgehead of Europe in Asia. It was also the foreland of the north Arabian steppe, from which its Semitic stock was constantly replenished when annual seasonal migrations of nomads for summer grazing after harvest became periodically mass settlement or armed invasion. Thus the Amorites settled at the end of the third millennium and the beginning of the second, and the great Aramaean tribal confederacies in the beginning of the Iron Age *c.* 1200. This common origin and the constant contact with the Semites of the desert hinterland was the great levelling influence, counteracting the diverse ethnic elements and cultural influences in Canaan. *Fig. 1*

The influence of Mesopotamia is early reflected in Sumerian seal-impressions on pottery at Megiddo in the fourth millennium and in the distinctive painted pottery (Tell Halaf and Ubaid ware) in the same period from the lower Orontes Valley and at Ras Shamra (Levels IV and III). The extent of the penetration of the West (*Amurru* or 'the Amorite land') by Sargon of Akkad (twenty-fifth century), who in his Omen Texts sweepingly claims the conquest of 'the land of the sunset and the mountains of cedar, all of it,' is vague, but it is highly probable that in this first imperial period of Mesopotamian history Sargon should have crossed the narrow land-bridge between the Euphrates and the sea in quest of the economic advantages of Syria, of which he mentions particularly the cedar, probably of the Amanus mountains. This interest is reflected in the Gilgamesh epic in the episode where the heroes kill Huwawa, the wild guardian of the cedar forests. Cuneiform tablets from Mari on the mid-Euphrates from the eighteenth and seventeenth centuries show the kings of the city-states of Yamkhad (Aleppo), Ugarit, Qatna, and Byblos in correspondence with the Amorite King of Mari. This correspondence also mentions Hazor in Palestine as an important commercial centre. Cylinder seals with Mesopotamian motifs and Akkadian legends from various sites in Syria and Palestine, from Ras Shamra, Qatna, Atchana, Tell Taʿannek, and Shechem in the Late Bronze Age attest the extent of Mesopotamian influence. The Amarna Tablets from the time of the Pharaohs Amenhotep III and Amenhotep IV (Akhnaten) with Egyptian officers and native vassals in Canaan (*c.* 1411–1378) prove that Akkadian was the *lingua franca* of diplomacy in the Near East including Canaan. The Canaanite princes must have had their local scribes and also teachers, as a certain tablet from Shechem may indicate. Akkadian exemplars are also implied, one such being almost certainly the myth of Adapa, the Sumerian story of how man forfeited immortality, which was found at Tell el-Amarna in Egypt, and a fragment of the Gilgamesh epic in Akkadian cuneiform found on the open ground near Megiddo in 1959. Thus Mesopotamian ideas gained currency in Canaan, where they were naturally assimilated as the dominant ethnic element in both areas since the end of the third millennium was Semitic, specifically Amorite.

Egyptian influence in Canaan is attested by material remains in strata of the third millennium at sites such as Byblos, Ras Shamra, Megiddo, and Ai near Bethel, also from funerary inscriptions from Egypt, and this evidence increases through the second millennium. The interest of Egypt in Canaan, apart from the turquoise and the limited amount of copper in Sinai, was the timber of the Lebanon. The Papyrus Golenischeff, which describes the misadventures of an envoy from Egypt in her weakness *c.* 1100, depicts Byblos as the chief lumber-port. Further evidence of this trade from early in the third millennium is provided by the copper axe-head belonging to an Egyptian lumberman, one of a boat-crew with an inscription naming Cheops, the builder of the great pyramid at Gizeh, which was found in 1911 near the mouth of the Nahr Ibrahim (the classical Adonis) near Beirut. Egyptian objects and a seal in archaic hieroglyphics from under the paving of a later sanctuary at Byblos indicate Egyptian interest in the local cult of the goddess of Byblos from *c.* 3000. Egyptian contacts reached inland also, to judge from certain Egyptian alabaster jars from the palace or temple of Ai at the end of the Old Kingdom. Eclipsed by Asiatic invasion during the last three centuries of the third millennium, Egypt recovered early in the second millennium to assert her authority in Canaan. Already in the twentieth century cordial relations between Ugarit and Egypt are attested by votive objects with the cartouche (honorific titles and designation) of the Pharaoh Sesostris I (1980–35) of the XII Dynasty found near the temple of Dagon at Ras Shamra. From this and the following century two royal sphinxes with the cartouche of Amenemhet III (1849–01) and statues of other Egyptian personages have been found in the vicinity of the temple of Baal, ostensibly votive offerings and marks of favour, but with the ulterior motive of impressing the natives with the power and splendour as well as the goodwill of the Pharaohs. Of peculiar interest is the seated sculpture of Khnumet-nofr-Hej (Khnumet of the Beautiful Crown), who is known as the wife of Sesostris II (1906–1887). By what seems more than coincidence the sphinx of another wife of the Pharaoh, the princess Ita, was found at Qatna about eleven miles north-east of Homs. Professor Schaeffer feasibly suggests that these were native Canaanite princesses whom the Pharaoh married as part of a regular policy, which the Pharaohs of the later XVIII Dynasty also practised on the evidence of the Amarna Tablets. A great

wealth of votive objects and presents in gold from the temples and royal tombs at Byblos in the nineteenth and eighteenth centuries further attest the influence and interest of Egypt. It is
Plate 1
particularly significant that the diadem of the king of Byblos is chased with such typically Egyptian motifs as the *ankh, was,* and *djed*-pillar, the symbols of life, well-being, and the renewal of kingship (respectively), and surmounted by the uraeus, or royal cobra.

Relations with the chiefs of Canaan, however, were not always so cordial. There were warlike tribesmen, whose arrival towards the end of the third millennium is marked by levels of destruction at archaeological stations throughout the land, as at Ras Shamra, Byblos, Hama, Bethshan, Ai, Jericho, Gezer, Askalon, Tell Beit Mirsim, Tell el-Hesy, and Tell el-ʿAjjul, and possibly Taanach and Megiddo. Two periods of dereliction have been noted, *c.* 2400–2300 and 2100–2000.

The first considerable documentary evidence of the Egyptian claim to the control of Canaan in the following period, the Middle Bronze Age (*c.* 2000–1600), are two lots of inscriptions, the so-called Execration Texts.

The first group, written in hieratic script, or stylized hieroglyphics, on vessels which had been broken as part of an execration rite of imitative magic, were unfortunately recovered out of their archaeological context, having been bought by an official of the Berlin Museum at Luxor, but have been dated on palaeographic grounds by the Egyptologist G. Posener to *c.* 1850. These texts name among enemies of Egypt a number of chiefs and localities in south Syria and Palestine. Not only do they indicate Egyptian interest in these lands, but they comprise the earliest documentary evidence for the ethnic identity of the people of Canaan and the nature of the settlement at the beginning of our period. The names of the chiefs are highly significant, being theophoric. In form they are identical with the Amorite, or proto-Aramaean, names of those who invaded Mesopotamia from the north Arabian steppe at the end of the third millennium and dominated it from *c.* 1800 during the First Amorite Dynasty of Babylon. To a large extent also they contain the same divine elements and the same attributes of the gods named as the Amorite names of Mesopotamia in this period. They are also identical in form with Hebrew proper names, especially those of the patriarchs, which generally take the form of the naming of God and the declaration of one of his activities or attributes by the juxtaposition of a noun, adjective or verb as predicate. We are thus at once introduced to the virile Amorite stock who forced an entrance into the Fertile Crescent in Mesopotamia and Syria from the north Arabian steppe, and at the same time to their gods and their peculiar conceptions of them.

Those Execration Texts further reveal the political and social organization of the Amorite inhabitants of Canaan and, we believe, their transition within the nineteenth century from tribes to settled communities. In the earlier texts from Luxor, for instance, several chiefs may be named in any one locality. Jerusalem, for instance, has two chiefs, Yaqir'ammu and Shayzanu, and Askalon three. This points either to confederate or autonomous tribes or perhaps successive waves of invading tribesmen, a view strikingly corroborated by the discovery of Dr Kathleen Kenyon at Jericho, that the invaders who destroyed the last Early Bronze Age settlement there practised simultaneously no less than five different forms of burial. The tribal organization of those people who are named in the Luxor texts and their provenance at no distant date from the steppes of north Arabia is further indicated by the fact that in their theophoric names their gods are termed their kinsmen, 'paternal uncle' (*'ammu*), 'maternal uncle' (*halu*), or 'father (*'abu*). This reflects the preoccupation of kinship groups with social relationships and responsibilities, on which the solidarity and the existence of the tribe still depends in the conditions of the desert. The fact that those people, who were to prove the dominant element in the land throughout the second millennium, settled the land thus as independent tribes, or at the most tribal confederacies, had a permanent effect on the history of Canaan. It contributed to that local particularism and lack of political cohesion which the physical diversity and limited resources of the land imposed on its inhabitants, and eventually left them an easy prey to a determined and unified aggressor like Israel and the large Aramaean tribal confederacies in the beginning of the Iron Age (*c.* 1200–1000). The peculiar nature of the Amorite settlement in Canaan conditioned the evolution of the small city-states in Syria and Palestine, which, after the introduction of the horse and war-chariot under the Aryans at the end of the nineteenth century became as hereditary fiefs the basis of Egyptian control of Canaan under the New Empire from the sixteenth century to the end of our period.

The second group of Execration Texts, on figurines acquired Plate 2 out of archaeological context in Cairo, but dated by Posener to *c.* 1800 on palaeographic grounds and by their relation to their probable provenance from a stratum of that period at Saqqara, witnesses to developments in the Amorite settlement. The kin-names of the deities in the theophoric names are notably fewer, the divine name Hadad being prevalent, with predicates which indicate that the worship of the peoples is now limited to given localities and directed to the problems of local agriculture. Hadad, of course, is now definitely known from the mythological texts from Ras Shamra as the god manifest in the storms and vital rains of late autumn and winter, the Canaanite Baal *par excellence*, the chief deity of the Canaanite peasant. The tribesmen were obviously becoming peasants (*fellahin*). A considerable degree of political unification had now been effected since generally only one chief is named in each locality. There is no evidence, however, that this unification was more than local, and indeed the congested settlements on their hill-tops or city-mounds with their fortifications out of all proportion to the size of the settlement bear witness to local rivalry, which has generally characterized the inhabitants of the land throughout history. This lack of cohesion and pre-occupation with defence stifled any cultural initiative in the inhabitants of those Canaanite settlements.

The settlements mentioned in the Execration Texts are to a large extent conjectural. Almost certain, however, are Askalon and Jaffa in the southern part of the coastal plain of Palestine, Aphek, which is probably to be located at Ras el-Ain at the source of the River Yarkon (Nahr Auja), Akko and near-by Achshaph, Byblos and probably Arka near Tripoli, Fihl (Pella) in Transjordan opposite Bethshan, Jerusalem and Shechem in the hills of the interior of Palestine, and possibly Iyyon, modern Merj Ayyun in Lebanon just beyond the Israeli frontier, and Hazor, the largest archaeological station in Palestine in the plain of the upper Jordan south-west of Lake Huleh. In addition Qarqar on the lower Orontes in Syria may be mentioned, though this is somewhat doubtful, and Yarmuth may be the place of that name in the Shephelah, or western foothills of Judah, just north of the Wadi es-Sunt, the celebrated Vale of Elah. Some 50 more localities are named, which are less certainly identified. Most of these may be feasibly equated, at least phonetically, with places of quite minor significance, mainly in the plains and western escarp-ment of Palestine, which appear mainly as names in the Old Testament in the tribal lists and localities in the Book of Joshua. *Fig. 2*

This at first sight suggests a rather sparse settlement, but the fact that certain sites such as Gaza, Megiddo, Bethshan, Jericho, and other sites in the plains of Palestine are not men-tioned, though they are known from excavation to have been occupied at this time, should warn us against concluding too hastily that the land was thinly populated in the nineteenth century as is often stated in passages on the patriarchal period in certain recent books on archaeology and the Bible. Nevertheless the beginning of the second millennium was for most of Syria and Palestine a period of slow recovery from the Amorite inroads and settlement which brought the Early Bronze Age civilization to a summary end towards the close of the third millennium.

An intimate sketch of those conditions in the Amorite settlement, probably in south Syria, is given in the Egyptian papyrus relating the adventures of the noble Sinuhe, a political refugee from Sesostris I (1980–35). After passing the chain of Egyptian forts in the Isthmus of Suez called the *Wall of the Prince*, Sinuhe was passed on from one district to another. This is just how you travel among tribes, one tribe guaranteeing your safety in its circuit and passing you on to another tribe with which it is on good terms. Probably this is a reflection of the piecemeal Amorite settlement which we have just described. Eventually Sinuhe settled with a tribe in 'the East' (*Qedem*). This has been taken as the steppe east of Palestine or Syria, but the description of that land as abundant in wine and olives points further west, since the olive does not flourish except in those parts of Syria and Palestine exposed to the Mediterranean climate. The fact that this fine agricultural region should have been the home of tribesmen in Sinuhe's time is just what the Execration Texts from Luxor lead us to conclude.

The Egyptian papyrus may be quoted:

It was a good land . . .
Figs were in it and grapes. It had more wine than water.
Plentiful was its honey, abundant its olives.
Every kind of fruit was on its trees.
Barley was there, and emmer wheat.

There was no limit to any cattle. . . .
Bread was made for me as daily fare, wine as daily provision, cooked meat and roast fowl, besides the wild beasts of the desert, for they hunted for me and laid (game) before me, besides the catch of my own hounds. . . .

Such natural assets, together with the timber of Lebanon, made Canaan a desirable sphere of influence, and after the Asiatic invasion in the First Intermediate Period at the end of the third millennium security demanded that Egypt keep the situation under control. Nevertheless Egypt experienced a second Asiatic invasion and domination *c.* 1730–1580. This was the period of the Hyksos. This term, actually *hyk khwsht,* meaning simply 'rulers of foreign lands', gives no clue to the ethnic affinity of the invaders. To judge from the distribution of pottery and royal scarabs distinctive of the period, and by their peculiar fortifications with their glacis advance-work to their city-walls, the Hyksos held Lower Egypt and Palestine and Syria in a unified command. Plate 3

In such a political movement it is natural to look for external impulses, but here the material evidence of the period, which might have been expected to furnish clues, is for the most part inconclusive. The sharp carination on new pottery types might indicate metal prototypes and point to an ultimate provenance in the metalliferous regions of Anatolia and the Caucasus. Metal vessels have been found in the royal tombs of Byblos (nineteenth century), but they came from Crete. A bronze belt with dagger attachment from Tell el-Farʿa by Nablus and another from Ras Shamra find their only affinities in the Caucasus. Plate 4

The most striking feature of this period is the appearance of the horse and two-wheeled war-chariot. It is believed that the horse, known in south Mesopotamia as 'the ass of the East', was introduced to the West by the Indo-Iranians; this is borne

Plate 5

out by the distribution of skeletons of horses and the remains of chariots and bits studied by A. Potratz. The first appearance of the horse in a settlement in Palestine is in the chalcolithic settlement (fourth millennium) at Horvat Beter by Beersheba, but it is not certain that the animal was domesticated. It next appears in burials at Tell el-ʿAjjul and Jericho in the Hyksos period, the custom recalling similar burials in south Russia and the Caucasus in the third millennium and the burials of horses and chariots with warriors in south Russia and east Europe associated with Aryans in the first millennium. The first mention of horses in Egyptian records is in the account of the expulsion of the Hyksos in the tomb of one of the notables who was a protagonist in the liberation. The first instance of equine remains in Egypt is from the eighteenth century at the great Middle Kingdom fortress of Buhen in the Sudan actually before the Hyksos period. E. Anati argues plausibly that the use of the horse and the light two-wheeled chariot originated in such terrain as the steppes of south Russia and the Iranian plateau, whence he would derive the Hyksos, whose characteristic defence works, the glacis and the moat, have north Syrian and Anatolian affinities. The large enclosure with earthwork glacis of the Hyksos period at Tell el-Yahudiyeh in the Delta has affinities with the fortified camps of the steppes of Turkestan. Emery's evidence of equine remains and the glacis fortification at Buhen before the Hyksos domination of Egypt modifies this view, though it is possible that the features may have been due to professional soldiers of the north recruited by the contending nobility in Egypt towards the end of the native Middle Kingdom. Also there is the fact that the words for chariot (*wrjt*) and its equipment in Egyptian texts are Aryan and that a text on horse-training from the Hittite capital at Boghazköi numbers the laps (*wartana*=turns) in numerals which have affinity with Sanskrit, e.g. *aika* (Sanskr. *eku*, 1), *tera* (Sanskr. *traya*, 3), *pansa* (Sanskr. *pança*, 5), *satta* (Sanskr.

sapta, 7), and *nawa* (Sanskr. *nava*, 9). This suggests that the population of Syria and Palestine was swollen and unsettled by the influx of the Indo-Iranians into the West at the end of the nineteenth century, where it is known that they succeeded in establishing a kingdom, Mitanni, between the upper Tigris and the Euphrates, and penetrated into north Syria. Other populations in north Mesopotamia and the Anatolian foothills, either conquered by the Aryans or displaced by them, became a prominent element in the population of Syria, where the Ras Shamra texts (fourteenth to thirteenth centuries) contain Hurrian texts and vocabularies and like the Amarna Tablets, attest Hurrian names in the army and among palace personnel. It is highly probable that the influx into Syria of these foreign elements, with the tactical advantage of great mobility in their war-chariots, gave the impulse to the invasion of the Delta, where Egyptian power was already disintegrating. The Amorites of Canaan, however, were also of fighting stock, and, with predatory instinct, would not be loath to join the foreigners in raids on the Delta. Eventually, as names on the scarabs of the Hyksos rulers show (e.g. Ja'qob-har and Anat-har), the Amorites came to supreme power, probably as the result of intermarriage with the Aryan and Hurrian military caste.

The chief consequences of this phase of history in the life of the Canaanites was the introduction of a feudal system with the advent of the horse and light war-chariot. Thus the rulers of the city-states of Syria and Palestine created a class of feudal barons of greater and lesser degree, on whom they settled heritable fiefs and privileges. This hierarchy of military specialists, whose rights and privileges depended ultimately on the king, is now well attested by legal texts from the chancelleries of Atchana and Ras Shamra in north Syria. It was adopted and adapted in Israel in the early monarchy (tenth century), but, running counter to the principles of democratic freedom native to the

Semitic tribes, it raised problems in the Hebrew administration, particularly after the incorporation of the Canaanite cities of the plains with their feudal society.

In 1580 Ahmes, the founder of the XVIII Dynasty of Egypt, defeated the Hyksos usurpers in the Delta, captured their capital Avaris, and expelled the foreigners, who, however, made a stand at Sharuhen (probably Tell el-Far'a in the Wadi Ghazzeh) for three years. For the next century Egyptian armies were active on repeated campaigns through Palestine and Syria, and even as far as the Euphrates. Here they encountered the kingdom of Mitanni. This well-organized state, where an Aryan aristocracy ruled over Hurrian subjects, effectively disputed control of north Syria with Egypt till it succumbed to Hittite diplomacy and aggression *c.* 1360. The Canaanite chiefs were ever ready to exploit this situation and to take advantage of the absence or temporary weakness of Egypt. Finally 330 of them under the leadership of the king of Qadesh on the Orontes concentrated at Megiddo to oppose Thothmes III in 1479. The Pharaoh, however, making a surprise dash through the famous pass of Megiddo from the coastal plain, won a complete victory in the field, though many of the chiefs escaped and Megiddo itself remained untaken for a number of months, a testimony to the strength of the Hyksos fortifications.

Thothmes' record of this campaign in the temple of Amon at Thebes (Karnak), as well as giving a valuable list of localities in Palestine, mostly known from the Old Testament, attests the material prosperity of Canaan in this flourishing period of her culture which resulted from the strong rule of the Hyksos. Costly vessels of silver and gold, chairs made from choice wood, objects carved in ebony and ivory, precious woods overlaid with silver and gold, and an elaborate statue of one of the notable chiefs of the Canaanites are listed among the spoils. In spite of the humidity of the soil in Syria and Palestine

Plates 6-16

and the frequent sack of cities, gold chased vessels, figurines in silver and bronze overlaid with gold, and carved ivory from this period at Ras Shamra, and indeed from Megiddo itself soon after, substantiate the claim of the Pharaoh.

One consequence of this campaign was that the Pharaoh took a number of chiefs and the relatives of others to Egypt as hostages. Nevertheless in the remaining 32 years of his life he led 16 more expeditions to Palestine. The fact that Egyptian inscriptions mention expeditions and the repeated removal to Egypt of great numbers of local notables as the regular pattern of Egyptian policy under Thothmes' successors, Thothmes IV and Amenhotep II, is a measure of the strong love of freedom in Canaan, which was no doubt fostered by Egypt's rival Mitanni in Upper Mesopotamia. The hostages, however, were treated honourably, and their experience in Egypt must have been generally a civilizing influence. Some indeed rose to positions of affluence and responsibility in Egypt, like Joseph in Hebrew tradition.

The extent to which the Egyptian domination affected the life of the Canaanites may be gauged from the fact that after a campaign in north Palestine and south Syria Amenhotep II (1448–20) records the deportation of 217 chiefs of *Retenu* (co-extensive with modern Palestine), 184 chiefs' brothers, 30,625 dependants of the deportees, 3,600 *'Apirw* (landless landlopers, who served mostly as mercenaries or serfs), 15,200 *Shasu* (nomads), 36,300 *Khurru* (Hurrians, possibly non-Semitic Syrians), and 10,600 subjects from *N'g's* (the region of Laish on the Orontes north of Hama).

But in spite of these periodic expeditions, the power of Egypt in Canaan was on the wane. Soon the Pharaohs no longer took the field in person, and employed in their armies and in the local garrisons not native Egyptians but Nubians and foreigners from the 'Sea-peoples' of the Aegean and the Mediterranean, the kindred of the Philistines. In the reign of

Amenhotep IV (Akhnaten) the reforming fantasy of this unpractical idealist involved Egypt in domestic tension and left the province a prey to anarchy, which is well attested in the diplomatic correspondence of the time between the Egyptian governors and native vassals in Syria and Palestine and the Egyptian chancellery in the new capital at Tell el-Amarna, the famous Amarna Tablets found in 1880.

These documents in Akkadian syllabic cuneiform, some 300 in number, dating from the reigns of Amenhotep III (1411–1375) and Amenhotep IV (1375–58), elucidate the condition, mainly from a political point of view, in contemporary Canaan. Besides letters from kings of greater powers such as Babylon, Mitanni, and the Hittites, with whom Amenhotep III particularly aimed at maintaining an *entente cordiale*, intermarrying with the royal house of Mitanni, the Amarna Tablets from Canaan are from Egyptian officials and local vassals, mainly of city-states already familiar from the older Execration Texts. We have already emphasized the political atomization of Canaan, partly the consequence of the physical diversity of the country, but more the result of the settlement of favoured sites by independent Amorite tribes or tribal confederacies. This local particularism is well attested in the Amarna Tablets. The King of Byblos, Ribaddi, the most loyal of the Egyptian vassals, for instance, accuses the King of Amurru (inland Syria) of disloyalty and duplicity, and complains that the King of Akko, who it is implied was less deserving, enjoyed more of the Pharaoh's favour. Tyre, by this time an island fortress, complains that Sidon is depriving her of water. The King of Megiddo accuses the King of Shechem of disloyalty to Egypt and open enmity to himself. The King of Jerusalem has also among his traducers his neighbour King Milkilu, probably of Aijalon, where one of the main valleys from the interior by Jerusalem debouches on to the coastal plain. There was no internal political cohesion among the Canaanites, a situation which facilitated the Hebrew settlement at the end of the thirteenth century.

These texts also illustrate admirably the reaction of natives to a suzerain power. They protest loyalty in the most extravagant terms. The King of Beirut, for instance, conforming to the conventional address, writes,

> To the King my lord, my sun, my god, the breath of my life . . . thy slave and the dust under thy feet. At the feet of the King my lord, my sun, my god, the breath of my life, I have bowed down seven times and seven times. I have hearkened to the words of the tablets of the King my lord, my sun, my god, the breath of my life, and the heart of thy slave and the dust under the feet of the King my lord, my sun, my god, the breath of my life, is exceeding glad that the breath of the King my lord, my sun, my god has gone out to his slave and to the dust under his feet.

Others declare:

> Who is thy servant but a dog?
> and they prostrate themselves before the Pharaoh
> Seven times and seven times on both back and belly.

The Pharaoh, however, was not deceived, and roundly threatened the King of Amurru, who seems to have cherished nationalist ambitions, with summary punishment. Indeed one King of Amurru, Aziru, was actually taken into custody in Egypt.

If it is true to say that most of the Canaanite chiefs of the Amarna Age resented the rule of Egypt, the situation had further complications. In Syria a definite nationalist policy seems to have been followed by the Amorites of the interior, notably Abdi-Ashirta and Aziru, though they, for all their apparent nationalism, were being exploited by the astute and ambitious Hittite King Shubbiluliuma, to whom one of the Ras Shamra texts records the tribute of the King of Ugarit and who raided as far as Byblos. Here in the North restless warrior groups appear, being designated in Akkadian ideogram SA.GAZ; these, on the internal evidence of the Amarna Tablets together with records from the Hittite capital Hattušaš (modern Boghazköi) and the recent evidence from the Ras Shamra tablets and others from the fifteenth century at Atchana (ancient Alalakh), are shown to be identical with the Khabiru. They are occasionally found acting on their own initiative, but in Syria they are more often unruly mercenaries of the chiefs who fought for Amorite independence, though certain of the loyal vassals of Egypt such as Namiawaza, probably of Damascus (Ubi), made use of the SA.GAZ in the interests of their suzerain.

In Palestine the situation was more complicated. There was no coherent policy of union against Egypt. The most notorious figures were apparently Abdi-Tirshi, the King of Hazor, and Labaia, probably the King of Shechem. The latter, whose name according to Ginsberg and Maisler is a common Hurrian type, made common cause with Milkilu, probably the King of Aijalon, whose name is Amorite. There are repeated complaints of these two aiding and abetting Khabiru invaders. Labaia in fact is accused of handing over his territory about Shechem to the marauders, indicating no doubt that he acquiesced in their settlement, a situation which may be reflected in the tradition of the settlement of Jacob and his family at Shechem (Gen. 33. 18–20; 34). With his accomplice Milkilu he raided towards the South, the territory of *Gazri* (presumably Gezer), Askalon, Lachish, and even the northern Negeb, or southern steppe of Palestine. But there is no indication of a combined nationalist movement. Labaia and Milkilu played for their own hand; the King of Hazor made common cause with the King of Sidon simply for the purpose of brigandage; Zutatna of Akko is accused of robbing a Babylonian caravan at Hinatuni on the ancient 'Way of the Sea' through Lower Galilee to the plain of Akko; Yapahi of Gezer complains that he is being ousted by his own brother, who has revolted and joined the SA.GAZ. Labaia lays siege to Megiddo but is captured by its king Biridiya, who hands him over to Zurata King of Akko to be shipped to Egypt. Zurata, however, frees Labaia for a bribe, and that reprobate is again at large to replenish his depleted resources by his accustomed brigandage. The whole action is on a mean and sordid scale, not worth recording were it not for the profuse references to localities in Palestine and the names of chiefs which indicate the complex ethnological situation in Canaan after the Hyksos invasion.

It is especially noteworthy that the Khabiru, who appear elsewhere in the Near East throughout the second millennium as mercenary soldiers or hired labourers or even as serfs, seem to be acting on their own initiative in Palestine. Of the gravity of this menace there is no doubt in the correspondence of Abdi-Khipa, the apparently loyal king of Jerusalem. This fact has led many scholars to equate the Khabiru of the Amarna Tablets with the Hebrews in the main invasion under Joshua. We disagree, though we recognize that the Khabiru, who possessed so much of the land by the right of the sword, surely made some permanent contribution to the population of which we should expect some trace in Biblical and extra-Biblical sources. Though texts of this period from north Mesopotamia indicate that Khabiru denoted a class rather than a race, it is conceivable that in Palestine the Khabiru were predominantly Semitic, land-hungry invaders from the Eastern steppes. Such Semites would easily coalesce with other Semitic elements already in the land such as Jacob-el and Joseph-el, to which the inscriptions of Thothmes III refer in the region of Shechem.

Plate 17

The Khabiru of the Amarna texts probably coincided with a certain number of those who later became incorporated into the Hebrew nation, but that certainly does not mean that the Khabiru inroads and the decisive phase of the Hebrew settlement traditionally associated with Joshua are to be exclusively identified. A synthesis of archaeological evidence from sites in Palestine, surface exploration in Transjordan, and the bulk of Biblical evidence suggests that the latter movement is to be dated over a century after the Amarna Age.

The Amarna Tablets and others of the same period from Taanach and Shechem in Palestine and contemporary administrative texts from Ras Shamra attest in their nomenclature a wide ethnic variety. In the Amarna tablets certain names are Amorite (e.g. Mutbaʿlu, Milkilu, Shammu'adda, etc.), others are Indo-Iranian (e.g. Shuwardata, Yashdata, Ruçmanya), and others again are Hurrian (e.g. Widia, Taddua, Abdi-Khipa, where the second element is the name of a Hurrian goddess).

Aryans in the Near East were first noticed in cuneiform texts from the Hittite capital at Boghazköi. In a treaty between Shubbiluliuma and Mattiawaza of Mitanni the gods of Mitanni–Mitra, Indra, Varuna, and the Nasatya twins – are invoked. This is a direct link with the Aryan vedas, where these gods are known. The kingdom of Mitanni in Upper Mesopotamia with its capital at Waššugani on a tributary of the river Habur, was a symbiosis of Hurrian subjects and an Aryan military aristocracy, whose power was based on a form of feudalism. The equestrian feudatories, *mariannu*, figure prominently in Hittite documents referring to Mitanni, and are now well known in tablets from the Late Bronze Age from Atchana and Ras Shamra. The word is connected with the Indic *maria* ('young man, hero'), the *marias* of the Vedas being the charioteers in attendance on the god Indra. The names of many of the *mariannu* in the texts we have mentioned confirm the Aryan connection. In Egyptian documents of the XVIII Dynasty they are found as prisoners of war in the Syrian campaigns and as professional soldiers, specifically charioteers. In Palestine proper among the names of the Amarna Tablets eleven at least are certainly Aryan, nineteen certainly Semitic, and three or four possibly Hurrian. The extent to which these non-Semitic elements were representative of the general population of Canaan is uncertain. They were probably feudatories placed in key positions where Egypt doubted the loyalty of native rulers, many of whom were removed with their families to Egypt. On the other hand the Old Testament apparently visualizes a mixture of ethnic groups in Palestine in the Late Bronze Age listing 'Hittites, Hivites' (for which the Greek translation of the Old Testament, the Septuagint, gives *Choraioi*, i.e. Hurrians), 'Perizzites, Girgashites', and possibly 'Jebusites' along with the Semitic 'Canaanites and Amorites'.

The Hurrians, first known through their peculiar names in cuneiform texts from Mesopotamia, where they were associated with the state of Mitanni, were further recognized in the records of the Hittites at Boghazköi as a definite ethnic element in the Near East from the vicinity of Lake Van in Armenia to Syria. Texts from Kirkuk and Nuzu about 150 miles north of Baghdad enabled Hurrian names in other texts to be more precisely determined, as in the Amarna texts and other tablets from the same period from Taanach and Shechem in Palestine. Hurrian texts and vocabularies were found among the Ras Shamra texts from the same period, and administrative texts demonstrate the extent of their influence in the feudal system of Canaan. As a result Hurrian elements are found distributed through Syria and the Orontes Valley to Palestine, being more numerous in the north. Whether there is any connection between these Hurrians, whom the Old Testament locates in Palestine and Edom, and the Egyptian name of Palestine,

Kkaru, remains an interesting possibility but an open question.

In spite of the mention of 'Hittites' in the Biblical description of pre-Israelite Palestine there is no evidence that the historical Hittites, who penetrated Anatolia probably from beyond the Bosphorus towards the end of the third millennium and ruled as an imperial power from *c.* 1900 to 1200, ever penetrated Palestine. Even at the zenith of their power under Shubbiluliuma (*fl. c.* 1370) their power did not extend beyond south Syria on the evidence of the Amarna Tablets and Egyptian records of the XIX Dynasty. 'Hittite' in the Old Testament is a geographic rather than an ethnic term, denoting a Northern race recognized as non-Semitic, probably Hurrian.

In the Amarna period and in the following century there is ample documentary evidence, especially from Egypt, that adventurers from all over the Levant were on the move, finding employment, as the *Šrdnw*, *Lwqw*, *Akhwš*, and *Dnyn*, as mercenaries of Egypt, the Hittites, and the Libyans. Indeed the restless activity of the Hittites at this time may have been largely owing to the numbers of these newcomers which Anatolia had to absorb. In Syria and Palestine, however, they are represented sporadically as mercenary garrisons, possibly attested in cremation burials at Atchana, Hama, Jericho, and Tell Beit Mirsim, a burial custom exceptional in the area since Chalcolithic times. But at the end of the thirteenth century the Philistines and their associated peoples came in force by land and sea down the Syrian coast, where they were halted by Ramses III early in the twelfth century in south Palestine, where he claims to have settled them as garrisons. On their way they destroyed such centres of Canaanite culture as Ras Shamra and Byblos.

Plate 18

Inference about the peoples of Canaan from nomenclature, however, must be used with caution. In the Amarna Tablets only the chiefs are named, placed in key positions doubtless where Egypt suspected the loyalty of the native rulers, whom they had no scruple in deporting wholesale with their families. Thus the non-Semites of the Amarna Tablets represent the ruling caste of a feudal order and were probably a minority. The case is justly presented by Professor Noth in an acute study of the administrative texts from Ras Shamra contemporary with the Amarna Tablets. Noting documents with relation to their provenance from respective parts of the city and with reference to the environment, status, and function of the bearers of the names, Noth has demonstrated that non-Semitic, chiefly Hurrian, names predominate in texts from the palace which refer to military orders, while in those which refer to the realm at large pure Semitic names predominate. This is precisely the situation implied in legal tablets from Taanach and Shechem about a century after the Amarna Tablets, where in some 100 names the proportion of Semitic to non-Semitic is 9:1. The sum of such evidence suggests that the main substratum of the population was Semitic. The non-Semitic minority consisted of military classes descended from Aryan and Hurrian professional soldiers who entered the land just before and during the Hyksos period, and heirs of their experience in chariot warfare and horse management, to which they owed their status and privilege. The influx of these non-Semitic feudatories probably increased with the Hittite domination of the politics of Mitanni towards the end of the Amarna period, occasioning the emigration of many of the ruling class, and it is significant that the great proportion of cylinder seals from Palestine at this time are of Mitannian design. Such seals, however, indicate persons of rank and office, hence a minority.

In the Amarna Tablets the weakness of Egypt is patent. The garrisons at key points throughout the land are small, and the appeals from the local vassals for reinforcements are modest, 10, 20, 30, and at the most 50 being the limit of their requests. Granted that these were meant only to secure Egyptian lines of communication pending the dispatch of large expeditions, it is significant that the desperate appeal of the loyal vassal Ribaddi of Byblos was met by the reply 'Protect yourself!'

The power of Egypt revived under the XIX Dynasty, Seti I (1313–92) and Ramses II (1292–25) particularly being personally active in repeated expeditions to Canaan, of which Egyptian records give an intimate picture. The scribe Hori, who was attached to the cavalry under Ramses II, in a scribal exercise for his pupils sketches the route of the Egyptian armies through Palestine, the muster and provisioning of the army on the desert frontier, and the various strategic points along the roads, Rafʿa, Gaza, Jaffa, Shechem, Megiddo, Bethshan, Tabor, Hazor commanding the fords of the upper Jordan, Achshaph and Akko in the coastal plain of Galilee, and other sites, the identity of which is less certain. The peculiar hardships of a campaign in Palestine are graphically described, the narrow rough passes where chariots had to be dismantled and transported on baggage animals, the rocks which cut the sandals to pieces, the thorns which rip the clothes, and the scrub which harbours hardy guerillas. The Bedouin are constantly pilfering, and night raids are made on the camp. Nor does the scribe omit the amorous adventures of troops encamped near the towns, who break discipline to visit houses of ill fame at the risk of their personal safety. The whole picture will strike a chord in the mind of all who served in the Palestine Police under the British Mandate. Such a land encouraged local independence, and the last case reflects the unpopularity of the suzerain power.

As early as the beginning of the second millennium Cretan
Fig. 4 wares are found at Ras Shamra, suggesting to the excavator C. F. A. Schaeffer that there were earlier contacts. In the Ras Shamra texts indeed *kptr*, or Crete, is associated with Egypt as

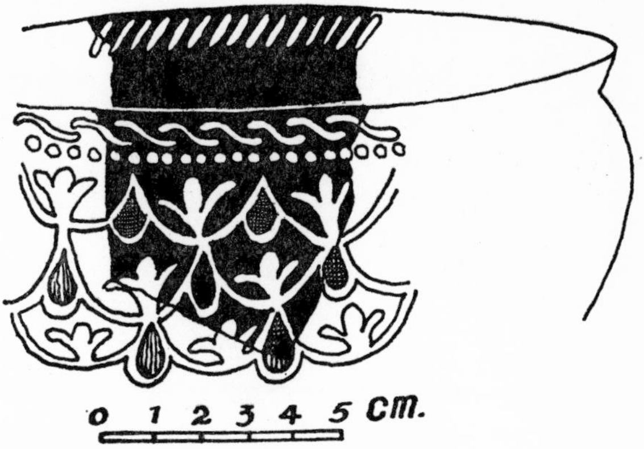

Fig. 4. Cretan potsherd, early eighteenth century from Ras Shamra (after Schaeffer)

the home of the arts. The Syrian coast was in fact a vital link between those early centres of culture. Now in the sixteenth century pottery with distinctively Mycenaean shape, technique, and decoration begins to pervade Canaan, indicating trade contacts, and there were actually Mycenaean trading settlements at Minet el-Beida, the harbour of Ras Shamra, and Tell Abu Hawam by the mouth of the river Qishon near modern Haifa, which date from the fifteenth century. The former settlement with its distinctive corbel-vaulted tombs of elaborate construction with definite Mycenaean affinities witnesses to the permanence of Aegean interest in this region, which, besides its native produce of wine, olive oil, and purple dye (*kinahhu*, Greek *phoinix*, hence Phoenicia), was a convenient entrepôt for the metals of Anatolia; it was frequented too by Mesopotamian merchants interested in those products and in the copper from Cyprus and the Taurus, as well as other merchandise from Egypt and the Aegean. Cyprus itself, readily accessible from

Fig. 5

Figs. 6, 7

Fig. 5. Aegean pottery types, Mycenaean and Cypriot, from the late Bronze Age in Canaan (after Barrois)

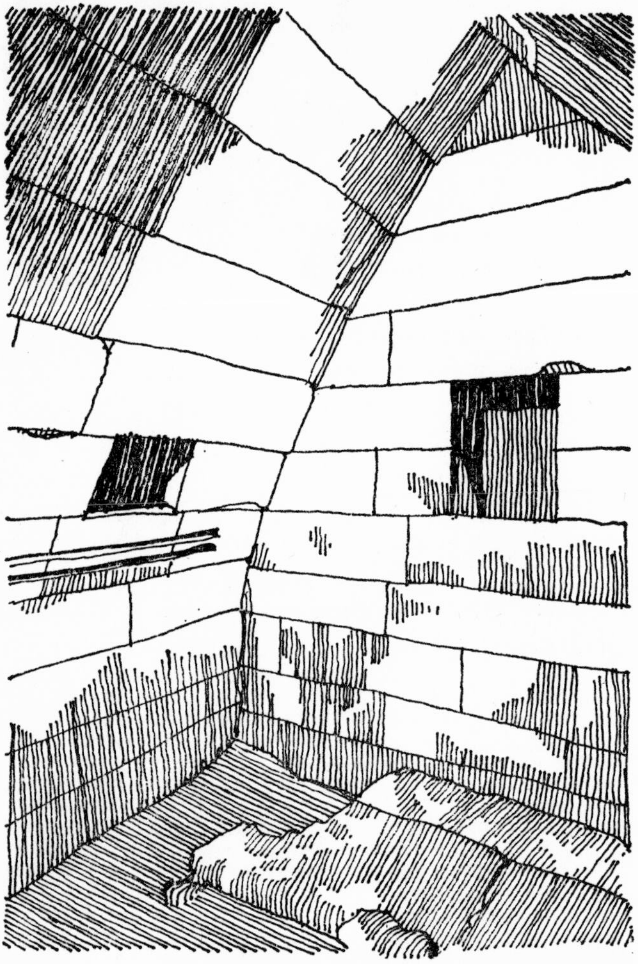

Fig. 6. Corbel-vaulted family tomb at Minet el-Beida by Ras Shamra. Late Bronze Age (after Schaeffer)

the Aegean and within sight of the Syrian coast on a clear day, was a constant attraction, and a potent influence on the culture of Canaan. From *c.* 1550 Cypriot wares are a commonplace in Canaan, both in inland and coastal regions.

Fig. 5

The campaigns of Seti I and Ramses II were directed against the Hittites, who had crossed the Taurus and captured Aleppo

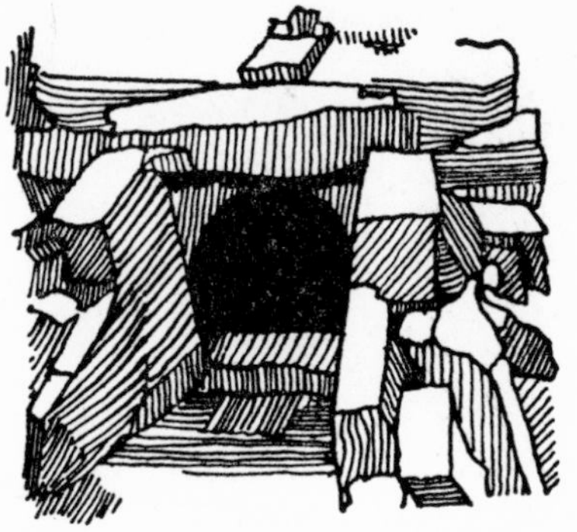

Fig. 7. Entrance to a corbelled family tomb at Minet el-Beida by Ras Shamra. Late Bronze Age (after Schaeffer)

c. 1460, and by the end of the fourteenth century had passed from diplomatic to armed aggression towards Palestine in proportion to the growing weakness of Egypt. Now Egypt with her administrative centre shifted from Thebes in Upper Egypt to the Nile Delta, where Pi-Ramesse (Tanis, Biblical Ramses, or Zoan) was rebuilt on the site of the old Hyksos capital of Avaris, maintained closer control over Canaan. The Canaanites were, as ever, susceptible to the intrigues and counter-intrigues of the major powers. In their frequent expeditions Seti and Ramses continued the policy of removing suspect notables for detention in Egypt. They also employed Canaanite mercenaries under the feudal system, and Egyptian papyri and inscriptions of the period, place-names such as Baal-Saphon and Migdol in the east of the Delta, and excavations at the site of Pi-Ramesse (San el-Hagar) all attest a dense Canaanite population in Lower Egypt and a certain pervasion even of Egyptian life and religion by Canaanite elements. Ramses II, for instance, entitles himself 'the companion of Anat and the Bull of Seth' – Anat being the Canaanite goddess of love and war, and Seth the Egyptian version of the Canaanite Baal – and sculptures of Canaanite deities, Baal, Reshef, Ashera, Anat, Astarte, and Horon are well known in remains of the period from Lower Egypt. Plates 19, 20

In spite of the enmity of the Canaanites and the movement of the restless Khabiru like those whom Seti repulsed near

Plate 21

Bethshan, as he states in his stele of 1313 from Bethshan, the ultimate enemy was the Hittites. Seti encountered them at Qadesh, and though he made a treaty with them hostilities broke out again. A great battle was fought in 1288 at Qadesh on the Orontes (Tell Nebi Mend) against the Hittites and their vassals from among the Canaanites of north Syria including Ugarit (*Ekeret* of the Egyptian inscription), which after almost a century of appeasement of both Egypt and the Hittites had had at last to commit herself. After a drawn battle a treaty was concluded delimiting the respective spheres of Egyptian and Hittite influence in Canaan at Qadesh. This permanently stabilized the situation between the two major powers until the collapse of the Hittites before the 'Sea peoples' from the Aegean coastlands and the Aramaean invasions from the Arabian steppe *c.* 1200, when the main phase of the Hebrew penetration took place. Then a new phase of history in Syria and Palestine begins with the powerful tribal confederacies of the Aramaeans, which eventually grew into national states.

In this connection the inscription of the Pharaoh Merneptah (1225–1215) in the beginning of his reign is of special interest. After recording his defeat of marauding 'Sea peoples' in the West of the Delta the inscription continues:

> Libya is laid waste,
> Heta (the Hittites) is at peace;
> Plundered is Canaan with every evil;
> Carried off is Askalon,
> Seized upon is Gezer,
> Yenoam is made a thing not existing,
> Israel is desolated,
> His seed is no more;
> Kharu (Palestine) has become a widow for Egypt,
> All lands are united in peace,
> Every land is fettered.

So ends the period of our study. From the close of the third millennium the Canaanites in their city-states had maintained their local independence with their own governments and institutions within the larger and rather loose fabric of empire, Egyptian, Hyksos, or Hittite. They had received various cultural influences, Egyptian in Palestine and on the Syrian coast, and to a lesser extent Mesopotamian, Hurrian, and Aryan in north Syria, the latter having revolutionized society with the introduction of the horse and chariot and the feudal order which that involved. Aegean influences had also borne on native Canaanite culture, particularly since the sixteenth century. But the Semites remained numerically the predominant element in the country and in consequence absorbed the other ethnic elements and their distinctive culture. This is noticeable in the native debasement of distinctive Canaanite wares towards the end of our period in the thirteenth century and in the predominance of the native Semitic dialect and the local nature-religion. For instance Egyptian influence is found in the representation of deities for whom the Egyptians recorded their veneration. The deities, however, in spite of their Egyptian guise and the hieroglyphic inscriptions are the familiar figures of the Canaanite fertility-cult, Seth of Saphon, Plate 22
Baal the lord of nature *par excellence* named after his royal seat on Mt Saphon – the commanding mountain over 5,000 feet high some 20 miles north of Ras Shamra – Anat his sister, Astarte, another fertility-goddess, and Reshef, who destroyed Plate 23
men in mass by war or plague. In spite of the political domina- *Fig. 8*
tion and the influx of foreign peoples, the *genii loci* of Canaan and her Semitic majority prevailed. The great political upheaval of the new Iron Age laid waste the Late Bronze Age cities of Ras Shamra, Byblos, Hazor, Bethel, Tell Beit Mirsim, Tell ed-Duweir and possibly Jericho. Now the Canaanites were absorbed in the new fiercely nationalistic states of the Aramaeans except on the Syrian coast, where the autonomous

Fig. 8. Stele dedicated by the architect Amen-em-Opet, shown with his son, to Mekal, possibly 'the Annihilator' Reshef, who slays men in mass by war or plague. His power of life as well as death is indicated by the ankh *(life-symbol) and* was-*sceptre (symbol of well-being). His identity with Reshef is suggested by the gazelle horns on his head-dress (after Rowe)*

Canaanite civilization was to flourish under the Phoenician merchant princes from the mountain barrier of the Lebanon and Alaouite mountains to the sea. But the culture of Canaan was to inform the thought and religion of the invaders, not least of Israel herself. Certain Canaanite elements were tacitly assumed and adapted. Others provoked violent reaction, especially from prophets and reformers, but assimilation had already gone far before reaction was expressed. In making possible a just assessment of the culture of Canaan and her permanent legacy to Israel, the spiritual progenitors of the Christian faith, the present study finds practical justification.

CHAPTER III

Daily Life

THE CANAANITE SETTLEMENTS familiar in the historical period originated generally in the beginning of the Bronze Age (*c*. 3000) on sites which were easily defended on some rock-spur or on an eminence in the plains, always by a reliable spring of water. Here the inhabitants built permanent rectangular houses and used the wheel to finish off their pottery. They also dug and lined pits for the storage of the grain they harvested in the plains with their serrated flint sickle-blades set in a handle of wood or bone – bronze, if not unknown, being still a monopoly of their imperial neighbours, and so scarce. The people generally relied upon the physical contour of the site for defence, but as the millennium progressed town walls were built, usually rude agglomerations of large unhewn stones or bricks such as might repel periodic nomad incursion from the east, as at Jericho, at Ai, where the pass from Jericho emerges on to the plateau north of Jerusalem, at Tell el-Farʿa at the head of the pass from the east up the Wadi Farʿa, and at Bethshan at the eastern end of the great central plain of Palestine.

After the unsettled period at the end of the third millennium associated with the coming of the Amorite tribesmen, the newcomers settled the old sites, which they eventually fortified still comparatively crudely, with walls of undressed or hammered stone set in clay mortar following the rock-ridge at the edge of the mound on which the settlement stood. Where those contours were not so pronounced, as at Gezer in the low foothills of Judah, the ramparts were more solid with towers set in the wall, which partly exposed the enemy to cross-fire. *Fig. 9*
This feature, with independent redoubts (*migdolim*) within the perimeter, was developed throughout the second millennium

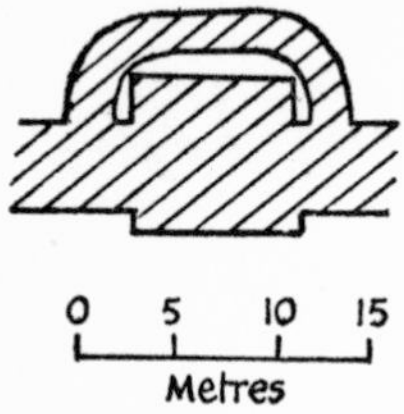

Fig. 9. Wall of Gezer with reinforcing tower, c. 2000 (after Barrois)

and became characteristic of Canaanite fortresses depicted in Egyptian sculptures (*c.* 1600–1100). The improvement in the facing and articulation of the city-walls was owing to the improvement of tools through the greater abundance of metal. Brick was also used, particularly in the superstructures. Many of the fortifications along the main highways of Palestine and Syria were vital links in the empire of the Hyksos, who expended the technical resources of that empire on their defence, from which the Pharaohs of the XVIII Dynasty benefited. While the fortification of such sites periodically subserved imperial policy, however, it was originally a symptom of local particularism, which we have noted as a feature of the land in all ages.

Plate 3

The glacis of beaten earth at an angle of about 30 degrees, occasionally with fosse and counterscarp dry, as at Lachish (Tell ed-Duweir), or filled with water, as at Qadesh on the Orontes, has already been noticed as a feature of fortification under the Hyksos. A further refinement which originated then was the heavily fortified city-gate either with direct entry through a double or triple barrier, as at Gezer, Ain Shems (Bethshemesh), and Shechem, or with a right-angled turn and three barriers, as at Tell el-Far'a by Nablus (probably Tirzah), where an Iron Age gateway reproduces features of gateways of the Middle and Late Bronze Ages. To reach this gate the assailants had to advance up the causeway on the glacis, exposing themselves to missiles from the wall above, usually on the right, the warrior's vulnerable side, the shield being

Fig. 10
Fig. 11

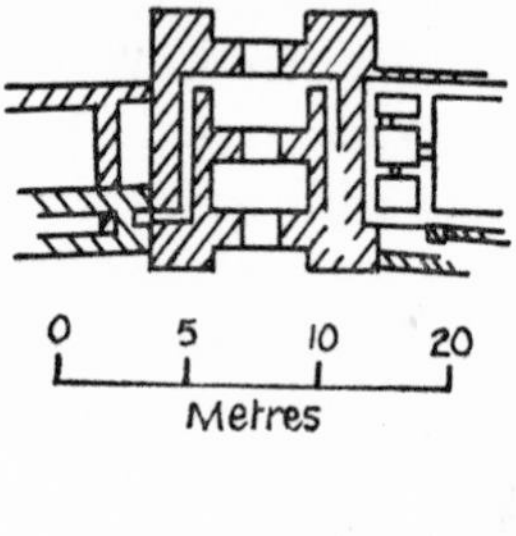

Fig. 10. Middle Bronze Age gateway at Shechem

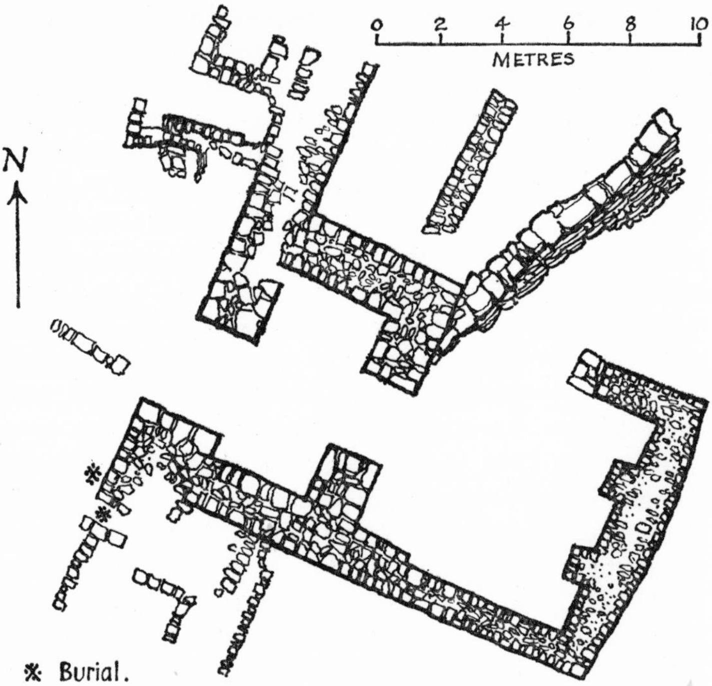

Fig. 11. Middle Bronze Age gateway at Tell el-Far'a by Nablus (after De Vaux)

normally carried on the left arm. After forcing the first barrier, a heavy wooden door plated with bronze and barred, and turning in a socket of hard stone, the assailants had then to fight their way through further barriers to the inner gate-chamber, often making a right-angled turn to the right.

The gates were double-storeyed and battlemented like the walls. A feature of the towers in the gate and the walls and of independent redoubts (*migdolim*) which has not survived at any site, but which is attested in Egyptian sculptures, is a projection of the upper storey by corbelling, which gave the defenders the same advantage as machicolation. Plate 24

The vital water might be a perennial spring, as at Jericho, Jerusalem, or Tell el-Far'a by Nablus. Such a spring was used for irrigation as well as drinking, but, being outside the wall, was vulnerable. Hence the city-wall might be extended to include the spring where the levels were suitable, or the water might be brought by tunnel within the defences, as at Ibleam (Khirbet Belameh) and Jerusalem, where the Spring of Gihon (Ain Umm ed-Daraj) was brought by tunnelling within the eastern wall of the pre-Israelite city, as the recent excavations of Miss Kathleen Kenyon and R. P. R. De Vaux have revealed. The water could be reached there by a sloping stairway and vertical shaft, the source being walled over and concealed. At Megiddo a great open shaft with a spiral stairway was sunk, to the bottom of which the water was brought through an inclined tunnel from the spring 70 yards away. Where there was no such spring wells were sunk to the water-table. This was usually within the city, as at Ras Shamra, Tell Beit Mirsim, Tell ez-Zakariyeh (Azeka), Tell es-Safi, and Bethshemesh, and access to the water-table might be provided on a grand scale by tunnelling a stairway through the rock, as at Gezer, and later at Gibeon (el-Jib). The well might be outside the walls, as at Lachish, where it is at the foot of the wall but at the top of the glacis, being driven 89 feet through rock to reach the water-table which was 112 feet below. These engineering works, even admitting the comparative softness of the limestone rock, are no small monument to the persistence and skill of the Canaanites, to the power of the local ruler to co-ordinate the efforts of his subjects, and to the intense local loyalty and determination to maintain independence against neighbouring city-states and periodic marauders from the desert.

Fig. 12

By the second millennium houses on these fortified sites were built rectangularly of clay or of bricks dried slowly and bound with clay mortar on stone foundations. The houses are generally

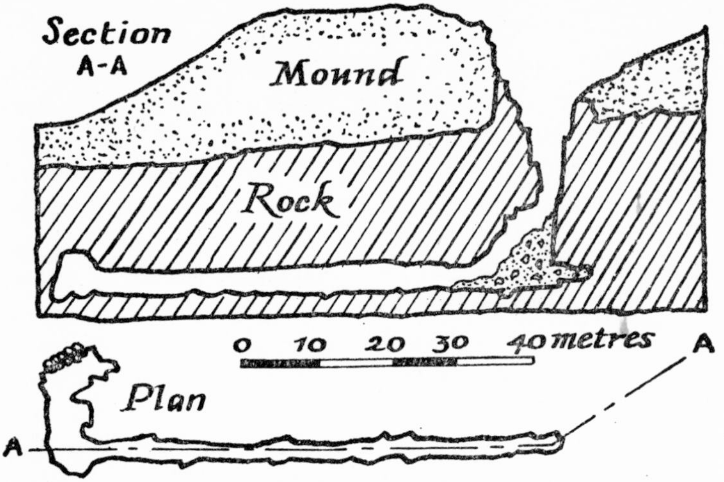

Fig. 12. Water-shaft and tunnel at Megiddo (after Kenyon)

small, the size being governed generally by the length of single timber beams which supported a light framework of timber or brushwood and a flat roof of rammed earth. The walls were protected against the weather by mud-plaster, and in the rainy season the surface of the roof, as still today, was kept unbroken by the use of a small roof-roller, which is occasionally found in excavations. Neglect of this domestic duty could cause serious annoyance, to which the Hebrew sage compares the railing of a nagging wife (Prov. 19.13), and a proper son is described in one of the Ras Shamra legends as one 'who plasters his roof on a rainy day'. For all this care, however, the brick walls absorbed a certain amount of water, which might cause some to disintegrate and the whole to subside under the increased weight. Against this danger apparently timber beams were set in the walls, a fashion of building which persisted even in stone-work, as at Ras Shamra in the Late Bronze Age and in Solomon's temple (I K. 6.36).

In warm climates, of course, much of the domestic work was done outside, as still in the villages of the East, and the house was essentially for the privacy of the family, though to be sure within the family circle there was little individual privacy. In winter a fire burned in an open hearth in the corner of the common room. Dried dung might be used to keep a smouldering fire alive, and for a more cheerful blaze in the short evening a bundle of thorns would no doubt be used, as at present. Within the common room a slightly raised platform (*mastaba*) at one end served as divan and family bed, and on the lower level the few simple kitchen utensils had a place, the grinding-stones, usually of the saddle-quern type, pottery cooking vessels, large storage jars for corn, wine, or oil, and the smaller water-pot.

In the Hyksos period the few residences of the patricians *Fig. 13* with their complex of rooms about a central courtyard walled off from the public street contrasted with the many cabins of the commonalty. In the courtyard a private cistern to collect rainwater from the roof and surface of the court, like that in which Jeremiah was imprisoned in the house of Malchiah (Jer. 38.6), was common, and here too there were generally also plaster-lined storage-pits (silos) for grain, and occasionally an enclosed baking-oven, with the quern and perhaps a mortar and pestle, usually of hard black basalt, for bruising olives. The larger houses, like the tent of a nomad sheikh, which must be large enough for public entertainment, had, besides private apartments (*haremlik*), one large hall (*selamlik*). This might be divided by several short stone pillars or bases for pillars of wood or brick to support more than one roof-beam. An excellent example is the large building, probably a palace, at Ai in the third millennium. Such buildings had often an upper storey, like the residence of the Moabite king Eglon (Judg. 3.20), but the flat roof served also for temporary guest-quarters or for the amenity of a social evening.

There is little if any evidence of town-planning. Building was sporadic, house being eventually joined to house within the confines of the ridge surrounding the top of the *tell* (city-

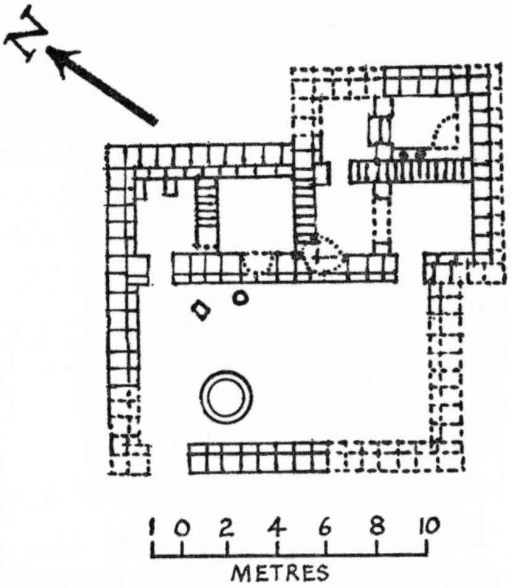

Fig. 13. Patrician house from the Middle Bronze Age at Tell Beit Mirsim (after Albright)

mound) till the settlement was a veritable warren. The streets, which were often *culs-de-sac*, were crooked and narrow, giving welcome shade from the fierce sun, but death-traps when the cities were stormed.

In these narrow, tortuous lanes, dusty in summer and miry in the rains, there was seldom adequate drainage. The main streets might be drained, as at Jericho in the Hyksos period. The Mycenaean quarter at Ras Shamra in the fourteenth and thirteenth centuries and patrician houses inspired by the Mycenaean model, quite exceptionally, had a bathroom in each house with drainage, with a sewer built of square stone slabs in the street by the palace. Generally, however, the town garbage accumulated at the door of the dwellings or immediately outside the walls to be scavenged by the dogs, which, as still in the East, made their nightly round (*cf.* Psalm 59.6).

These congested Canaanite cities were probably not unlike the old city of Jerusalem with its network of narrow, crooked streets and concentration of trades in their own quarters. The latter custom is attested in the Middle Bronze Age at Beth-shemesh, where the smiths' quarter was in the north-west of the settlement. Foreign merchants also doubtless had their quarters in the Canaanite cities along the trunk highways, as those of Damascus had at Samaria in the time of Omri (I K. 20.34).

The excavation of Canaanite cities shows no open spaces within except the courtyards of palaces, mansions, and temples. The place of public concourse was about the gate, to a limited extent inside, as within the present Damascus Gate in the old city of Jerusalem, but usually outside, where the converging tracks made a well-worn public place, Hebrew *goren* (*cf.* Arabic *el-jaruna*, 'the worn track', from *jarana*, 'to fray, rub'), the scene of administration by the ancient king Dn'el in the Ras Shamra legend, which states:

> He rises to sit at the entrance of the gate,
> In the place of the notables (*tht 'adrm*) who are in the public place (*dbgrn*).

Again an illustrative modern analogy is the Damascus Gate in Jerusalem with its coffee-halls, money-changers, and professional scribes and notaries. An excellent case of the public place within the city-gate of a Canaanite city is that of Tell el-Far'a by Nablus in the second phase of the Middle Bronze Age (nineteenth century).

This instance is interesting as producing a possible case of the gruesome custom of human sacrifice on the building of the gateway, to which I K. 16.34 may refer in the account of the rebuilding of Jericho by Hiel the Bethelite,

> He laid the foundation thereof in Abiram his first-born, and set up the gate thereof in his youngest son Segub.

Fig. 11 In the open space within the gate of Tell el-Far'a the skeletons of two new-born infants were found buried in jars with smaller pots of the Middle Bronze Age (*c.* nineteenth century). Since these were not associated with other burials in private houses but were isolated, they may well have been special sacrifices. The gate, like the door and threshold of a house, is one of those intermediate areas which, like intermediate periods of time or critical phases of life, the primitive mind invests with a peculiar significance as the point at which the subject is especially vulnerable to supernatural agencies. Hence we find rites associated with the doorway common among primi-tive Semites, e.g. the blood-smearing rite of Passover in ancient Israel and the sacrifice of an animal among modern Arab peasants at the door of a new house. Burials of infants under the thresholds of Canaanite houses and anthropomorphic figurines of bronze and silver under house-foundations at Gezer point to the same superstition, a modification of the rite being the deposit of a lamp and inverted bowl under the threshold in the Iron Age, even among the Israelites.

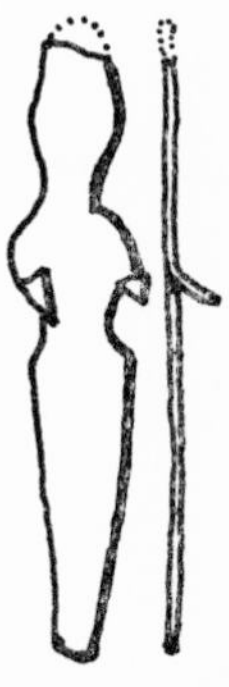

Fig. 14. Foundation figurine from Gezer (after Macalister)

What of the palaces of the Canaanite kings of the Amarna Tablets? In view of the limitation of their royal status and of the fact that their realms seldom exceeded a radius of 20 miles we should not expect great splendour. At Jericho, Bethel, Tell Beit Mirsim, Tell el-ʿAjjul, Bethshan, and Hazor in Palestine in the Middle and Late Bronze Ages any of the larger two-storeyed houses built around its courtyard could be the 'palace'. At Megiddo in Level VIII (fifteenth century) such a building by the city-gate around several courtyards covering some 1,500 square yards may have been the palace, as the rich hoard of gold, ivory, and lapis lazuli under the floor of one of the rooms suggests. The celebrated ivory from Level VI A (*c.* 1200) depicting the king on his throne re-ceiving prisoners of war to the accompaniment of music and dancing suggests something of the royal estate of the Canaanite kings. Megiddo, however, was one of the strategic centres of Palestine for Egypt, and no doubt profited from the trade and

Plates 11–15

Fig. 15

Fig. 15. Incised ivory plaque from Megiddo c. *1350–1150, with two scenes of the king returning from a campaign and the king on his throne receiving tribune (after Loud)*

culture of the Aegean merchant colony at Tell Abu Hawam some 10 miles distant.

The palace of the Canaanite king, like that of Solomon in Jerusalem, might include one or more sanctuaries in its complex, as does that of Qatna, where a small shrine and a large temple of the Moon-goddess Nin-gal were incorporated with the palace with its public and private quarters grouped around two courtyards in a complex of 8,400 square yards.

What royal estate could be in Canaan of the Late Bronze Age even in a small city-state is seen in the palace of Ras *Fig. 16* Shamra. With its 67 rooms arranged about five courtyards this palace so far recovered covers an area of over 10,000 square yards. It was of course more than a private residence and four separate quarters were reserved for business and state archives, which have yielded a rich harvest of administrative and legal texts in local alphabetic and Akkadian syllabic cuneiform tablets. An entrance from the west, dominated to the south by a *migdol* (tower) and flanked by two wooden pillars 5 m. apart on stone bases 1 m. in diameter, gave access through a stone-paved portico to a reception-chamber, off which a small door led to the treasury-offices, where a great number of official dockets were found with a bronze stylus of the scribes. A wide entrance to the right, flanked at the right by two sentry-niches, where arms were found, gave on to a stone-paved court (I), in which there are marks of chariot-wheels. Here there was a

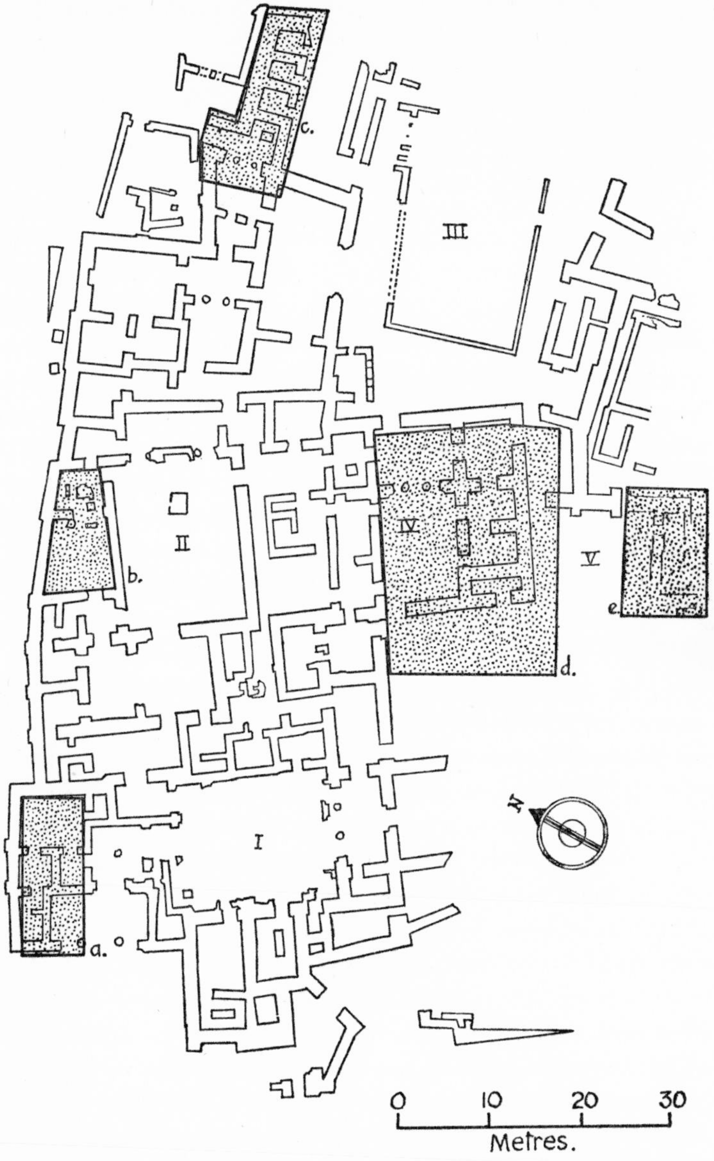

Fig. 16. Plan of the palace at Ras Shamra at the end of the Late Bronze Age, c. 1200*; areas a, c, d, e, archives; area b, royal burial-vaults (after Schaeffer)*

well and a trough, the former being covered by a well-fitting stone and neatly lined with masonry, which was still intact, water being actually found at a depth of 11 m. which thereafter supplied the wants of the expedition.

At the south end of this court a large colonnaded vestibule still admitted the chariot of the king, but from this point the interior was accessible only on foot. Beyond a series of halls another interior court was reached, but the fact that east of this point the palace complex extends for the same distance on a lower level indicates that the whole palace as it was used at the end of the Late Bronze Age was not conceived on a single plan, but grew piecemeal. North of the large court the royal burial-vault was found with three subterranean chambers with ossuary-niches. The graves are corbel-vaulted chambers, approached by descending steps covered by large flat stones. In the Late Bronze Age at Ras Shamra Mycenaean cultural influence, so strong elsewhere in the city, extended to the palace itself.

Three more interior courts and three independent suites of rooms reserved for administrative business were uncovered. One suite was situated at the north-east entrance to the palace, which, to judge from the texts, dealt with business, legal and mainly fiscal, concerning the city and its immediate suburbs in contrast to the department by the west entrance, which dealt with business from the country districts. Another was located off court IV in the middle of the palace. This was where the more intimate business of the royal house was transacted. The texts here were mainly legal, dealing with gifts and conveyance of property, adoption, etc., a large proportion of them being sealed with the royal seal of the reigning dynasty. A small department separated from the last by a small interior court dealt apparently with external political business, to judge from the political documents in Akkadian found here, some of which bear the seal of the Hittite royal house.

The palace of Ugarit still impresses even though no more than part of the plan remains. Complete with its upper storey or storeys, which eleven stairways indicate, furnished with fine wood, metal-work, and carved ivory panelling, garrisoned by the royal life-guards, scribes busy in the various departments of the chancellery, foreign diplomats and any who had business thronging the vestibules and interior courts, to say nothing of the household staff and the king and his family and entourage passaging in their chariots out and in by the west entrance and outer courts and colonnaded vestibules, this must have been most imposing.

No palace of comparable size and wealth has been found in Syria or Palestine, and it is almost certain that none such existed. Ugarit was quite exceptional and was a wonder in Canaan, as the King of Byblos, itself no mean city, indicates in his letter to Amenhotep IV. At the cross-roads of trade-routes from Mesopotamia, Anatolia, Canaan, Cyprus, Crete, and the Aegean, and Egypt with her various products, Ugarit was a vital factor in the delicate situation and eventual strife between Egypt and the Hittites. Easily accessible from Egypt by sea and from the Hittite homeland in Anatolia by land, Ugarit was courted by both, who seemed to have valued her voluntary support and her economic significance too highly to have ventured on conquest and occupation, a situation which the kings of Ugarit were not slow to exploit. Moreover this favoured site was the earliest refuge for the refugees from Crete, Cyprus, and the islands in the first phase of the activity of the sea-rovers who destroyed the Minoan power and burned the palace of Knossos *c.* 1400. Ugarit was in consequence greatly strengthened by the access of the wealth and technical skill of the Aegean people, to which the corbel-vaulted tombs of the kings, notables, and wealthy citizens of Ugarit bear eloquent witness in the Middle Bronze Age and particularly in the last century of the Late Bronze Age. The administrative tablets from the palace archives show that the king of Ugarit at that time, as well as being feudal head of the realm, was a merchant prince who derived rich dues from overseas trade.

A conspicuous feature of the Canaanite city was the holy place. Here unfortunately the archaeological evidence is often open to subjective opinion, and with this reservation we offer the following analysis of evidence. We should discriminate between the shrines of the gods of the settled land and the holy places venerated through association with the ancestors of the community, where, usually by a sacramental meal or a sacrifice, the solidarity of the community or clan was effected and maintained.

The latter holy place was, we believe, the primitive sanctuary of the nomad, who still venerated the burial-place of his tribal ancestor. These would be the first sanctuaries of the Amorite tribes, men who settled the land *c.* 2000. Such was, we believe,

Fig. 17

the famous 'high place' of Gezer. There eight and possibly eleven limestone monoliths stood in a gentle crescent aligned for some 30 yards roughly north–south on a raised platform of squared stones except one which was set in a stone socket. This raised platform, we believe, is the 'high place' (*bamah*) proper so often mentioned in the references to unorthodox provincial worship in the Old Testament. Before two of these was a large limestone block 6 ft 1 in. by 5 ft by 2 ft 6 in. with a square-cut depression 2 ft 10 in. by 1 ft 11 in. by 1 ft 4 in. deep. The fact that this shows no sign of plaster-lining has been taken to rule out its use as a container for liquid, and it has been suggested that it was the socket for a pillar of wood which represented the mother-goddess Ashera. But the limestone could still have contained a thick fluid like blood from the sacrifice for the brief time that it was needed to sprinkle the worshippers and the symbols of the supernatural to effect communion. The sacred significance of the area at Gezer is indicated by the burials of young infants in jars in the subsoil,

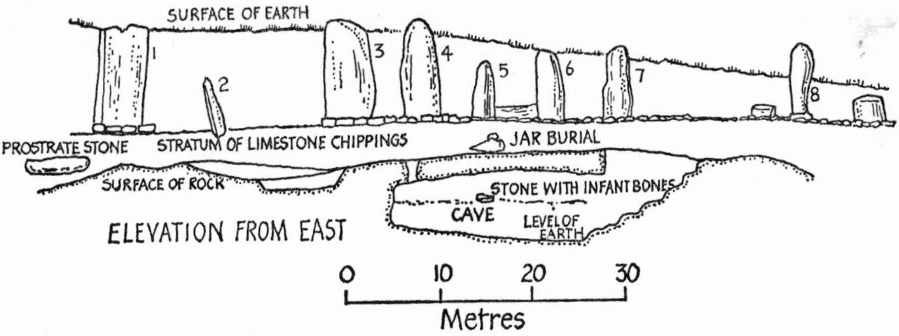

Fig. 17. Open-air sanctuary at Gezer (after Macalister)

the pottery indicating the middle of the second millennium. On the analogy of similar jars with infant skeletons filled with intrusive sand at Tell el-Hesy the excavator R. A. S. Macalister supposes that the infants were smothered with earth. These remains, almost all of infants a few days old, are conceivably the offering of the first-born, either in fulfilment of a vow or a crude version of the Hebrew conception that the first-born males of man and beast were dedicated to God (Ex. 13.1–2; 22.28–29) and were to be redeemed by an offering (Ex. 13.11–15; 34.19–20). In the same complex were two caves with steps leading down to them; these were used as dwellings in the Chalcolithic period, but were later joined by a crooked passage and used possibly for oracles in conjunction with the sanctuary. The standing stones (*masseboth*) which the Old Testament associates regularly with the 'high places' (*bamoth*) are conceivably memorials of great ones among the ancestors of the community who had manifestly possessed the divine favour (*beraka*) and who, as in primitive Arab society, are the patron saints (*welis*) of the people. Small pillars in the Late Bronze Age temple at Hazor may have a like significance. A relief on one of those of two hands stretched up to a disc within a crescent may indicate the intercessory function of the dead

Plate 26

kinsman, whose presence was symbolized in the pillar. In this connection one of the Ras Shamra texts notes the significance of the son of the king as

> One who may set up the stele of his ancestral god (*'el'ebh*)
> In the sanctuary which enshrines his forefather.

Such standing stones on the other hand might be memorials of theophanies, as the pillar which Jacob set up and anointed at Bethel (Gen. 35.14–15), which is probably the significance of the congestion of such pillars in the 'Obelisk Temple' at Byblos from the first half of the second millennium. (Plate 25)

Bamoth in the Old Testament, which often means such a sanctuary as that at Gezer including memorials of dead kinsmen and more specifically the raised platform on which they stood or the burial mound itself (*cf.* Ez. 43.7, Isa. 53.9 in the Qumran text, and Job 27.15 with a change of vowels), signifies also a raised and levelled mound either for hecatombs or to accommodate an altar. The classical example is the great drystone mound at Megiddo in conjunction with the three Middle Bronze Age temples (*c.* 1900). (*Fig. 18*) Slightly oval, it still stands *c.* 6 feet high and from 8 to 10 yards across with a flight of seven steps and enclosed by a wall. A similar feature has been discovered at Nahariyeh 6 miles north of Akko in conjunction with a small sanctuary of the early Hyksos period (*c.* 1700). This mound was originally rather smaller than the Megiddo *bamah*, but was later enlarged.

For antiquity and length of service the shrine of the Lady of Byblos takes pride of place. Originating in remote antiquity, as Dunand believes, in the cave still preserved in the paved precincts of later buildings, the sacred precinct received a built temple early in the third millennium under Egyptian patronage. Foundation deposits, which include Isis figurines, fix the next phase to the beginning of the second millennium.

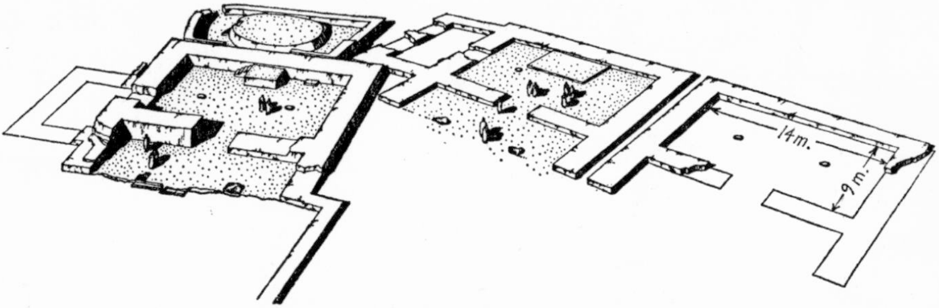

Fig. 18. Megiddo 'high place' of the Middle Bronze Age (after Loud)

This sanctuary, of which the large open precinct was the permanent feature, resembles on a much smaller scale the Muslim Haram esh-Sharif at Jerusalem, where worship began probably at the famous rock with its cave under the present Dome in remote antiquity and has continued with built sanctuaries and sacred foundations in the holy precinct for almost three millennia. In the sacred area of the goddess of Byblos as repaved and rebuilt *c.* 2000 BC foundation deposits indicate that a certain chamber may be the 'holy of holies' and three huge blocks of roughly dressed stone approached by three steps almost certainly formed the altar. These two features were located in a part of the precinct to which the public had probably no admittance.

Specifically associated with the sedentary life in Canaan were built temples, which symbolized the presence of the gods. Those were conceived of as houses (*battim*) of the gods and consisted in essentials of a room for the god, whose presence was symbolized by a statue or some sacred symbol, with other compartments for priests and worshippers. Here we must emphasize local variations in the plan of those temples. The form might be a single broad compartment with direct access from a portico directly opposite the platform for the divine symbol or the altar, as in the three Middle Bronze Age temples by the great *bamah* at Megiddo. In the Late Bronze Age shrines *Fig. 18*

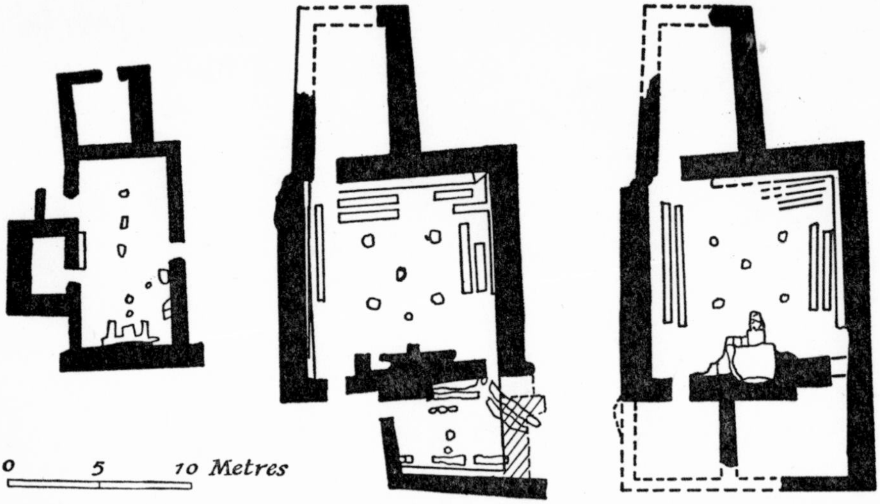

Fig. 19. The Lachish temple beyond the city wall with two later reconstructions in the Late Bronze Age (after Starkey)

Fig. 19 at Tell ed-Duweir (fifteenth to thirteenth centuries), Bethshan VII (thirteenth century), Tell el-Far'a by Nablus, and Hazor
Plate 27 the access is indirect through an antechamber, the altar and its symbol on the raised platform at the back of the shrine being screened from the vulgar view. In the temples of Baal and
Fig. 20 Dagon at Ras Shamra, which were in use from *c.* 2000 to the end of the thirteenth century, access was from one of the longer sides into a forecourt, where the great altar stood, the inner court and 'holy of holies' being thus well screened. Not only do the plans of these temples vary from locality to locality, but apparently the principle of one temple for one god was not *de rigueur*. At Megiddo in the Middle Bronze Age for instance the single dais or pedestal in each of the three temples by the
Fig. 18 great *bamah* indicates that each was dedicated to a single deity.
Fig. 19 At Tell ed-Duweir on the other hand the small shrine of the Late Bronze Age in the Hyksos fosse outside the city wall, which was rebuilt twice before its final destruction *c.* 1230, has at the back a long dais with three projections in front, apparently altars. The worship of a triad, possibly El and

Ashera, the Creator and the Mother-goddess, and Baal-Hadad, the young vigorous god primarily of rain and storm and secondarily of vegetation, was apparently concentrated in this one temple, as the worship of the male Mekal and a female deity was concentrated probably in the earliest sanctuary at Bethshan (late fifteenth and early fourteenth centuries). Those shrines were quite small, that at Megiddo measuring about 25 by 15 yards and the largest of the Lachish shrines, the latest reconstruction, roughly the same on the outside. These, however, were the actual shrines which housed the divine symbol and were used for the consulting of oracles, and possibly ritual incubation, and certainly for the deposit of offerings, which were laid on stone or clay benches round the walls, as is indicated by the many storage jars found in the shrine of Tell ed-Duweir (Lachish). Much of the surrounding area outside was used for the assembly of the community on religious occasions, as was the outer court of the tripartite temple which eventually evolved.

The temple of Baal at Ras Shamra, somewhat larger than that of Dagon at the same site, which was built on the same general plan, had an external measurement of 40 by 20 m. It clearly reveals the tripartite plan best known from Solomon's temple at Jerusalem. Orientated north–south, the temple at Ras Shamra consisted of an outer court with an altar measuring 2.20 by 2 m., a narrower and smaller court, and the inmost shrine, shallower but broader, which no doubt contained the divine symbol. Indirect access was from the west side to the junction of forecourt and inner court, and a corridor ran from the north along the east side, giving access to the outer court opposite the altar. It is thought that the corridor served as an entry for sacrificial beasts. *Fig. 20*

What has survived of the furniture of those temples is simple, but the cuneiform inventories of the treasures of the temple of the Moon-goddess Nin-gal at Qatna remind us that it was not

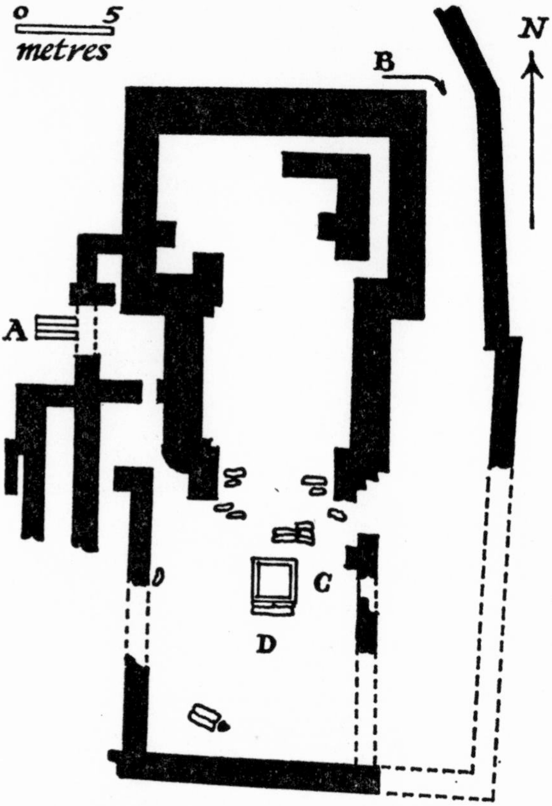

Fig. 20. The Baal temple at Ras Shamra from the Middle to the Late Bronze Age. A. Priests' entrance; B. entry for sacrificial beasts; C. altar; D. forecourt (after Dussaud)

always so. Among a great weight of gold objects, certain of which are not yet identified, these texts from the middle of the second millennium list an image of the goddess in red gold with an object of yellow gold in her hand, the whole weighing 10 shekels, two large gold eagles, one gold bull, and six gold thrones. In our assessment of Canaanite art it is to be deplored that the head of a lion in (rock) crystal set in gold and that of a bull's head in lapis lazuli set in gold have not been recovered. The dais or pedestal points to an image, though nothing of the kind of any size has been found in Palestine or Syria except in the Late Bronze Age temple at Hazor, where the figure of a male deity 40 cm. high, sculptured rather roughly in local black basalt, is seated on a throne holding a cup or bowl for offerings. The inverted crescent on the breast of the figure indicates, on the analogy of the Sumerian ideogram, the Moon-god Sin, and it is significant that one of the accompanying standing-stones exhibits the disc and crescent as the object of two hands uplifted in prayer. In view of the stormy history of Canaan, the involvement of Syria in repeated rebellions and punitive raids by the Assyrians, and periodic reformations in Israel and Judah, we need not expect the survival of large images of gods, and in fact the head of the Hazor figure had been broken off. Stelae, however, with reliefs of the gods were found at Bethshan and Ras Shamra. The whole stele is usually less than 50 cm. high, but that of Baal with the lightning-spear from the first half of the second millennium at Ras Shamra stands almost 1½ m. high. The appearances of such images may be further visualized from figurines of deities, probably *ex voto* offerings or images cast from temple-offerings for sale

Plate 26

Plate 23, *Figs. 8, 21*

Plate 28

Fig. 21. Stele with a relief of a god and worshipper, probably the king. The aged god in repose is thought to be El, the senior god of the Canaanite pantheon, as known from the Ras Shamra texts. His horns have been thought to reflect one of his stock epithets tr'el *(the Bull of El) but they are also the symbols of various gods in the Semitic East (after Contenau)*

Fig. 22. Figurine of Baal from Ras Shamra, copper inlaid and overlaid with gold and silver (after Schaeffer)

Figs. 22, 23

Fig. 8

Plate 19

by the priests, usually in bronze and occasionally overlaid with gold and silver, from the Late Bronze Age at Ras Shamra, Megiddo, and Tell ed-Duweir. Such figurines from Ras Shamra and Minet el-Beida reproduce the attitude of Baal on the stele we have mentioned. Figurines of the warrior-god like Baal may be Reshef, who, we think, is represented as Mekal (Hebr. *mekalleh*), 'the Annihilator', in a stele from Bethshan. This is suggested by the motif of the gazelle-horns which adorn the headgear of the god and by the fact that Bethshan by the Nahr Jalut is a notoriously malarial region. The goddesses of the fertility-cult are similarly known from reliefs on

Fig. 23. Figurine of Baal from Ras Shamra, copper inlaid and overlaid with gold and silver, Late Bronze Age (after Schaeffer)

stelae from Bethshan and Ras Shamra, and from nudes in terracotta and gold pendants from nearly every major Canaanite site in the Late Bronze Age. Plates 29, 30

The standing-stone (Hebr. *massebah*, which, however, may also mean a free-standing image), as well as being a memorial of the dead, might be a cult-symbol marking the site of a theophany, the place where the presence of the god was realized, like the stone set up by Jacob at Bethel (Gen. 28.18; 31.13). This may possibly be the significance of the many stelae in the Obelisk Temple at Byblos. The *massebah*, whatever its significance in the cult, was associated particularly Plate 25 with the male deity. The symbol of the Mother-goddess was the *asherah* (lit. 'upright'), which we now know from the Ras Shamra texts to be the name of the Mother-goddess, the consort of El and the mother of the divine family. This word is often translated in the Old Testament as 'the grove', suggested by the fact that it could be uprooted (Mic. 5.13; II K. 23.14), cut down (Judg. 6.26) and burned (Deut. 12.3; II K. 23.6, 15). It was of wood (Judg. 6.26) and might be an actual tree planted by man (Deut. 16.21). Generally, however, particularly in the shrines in the Canaanite cities we have mentioned, the tree was stylized in a wooden pole or trunk which probably stood in a socket in a stone base, as in the first Canaanite temple excavated by Rowe at Bethshan. This may have been the purpose of the stone socket which we have noticed in the 'high place' at Gezer and in the similar stone socket in one of the temples of the period at Byblos. The tree probably represents the life-principle fostered by the rain, which was the province of the male god Baal-Hadad. It is possibly represented in the tree of life, naturalistic or stylized, flanked by caprids, which is a common motif in Canaanite art. In this Plate 32 connection the goddess seated between the two caprids to which she offers plants on the ivory unguent-box from the Late Bronze Age at Ras Shamra suggests the connection between the fertility-goddess and the sacred tree.

Incense was burned in perforated bowls which fitted on top of hollow perforated stands of pottery or bronze, square or cylindrical. These might be modelled as a multi-storeyed house or shrine with windows, as the specimen from Bethshan (eleventh century), and usually had figures superimposed, such as sphinxes and lions, as in the stand from Taanach, or serpents. Birds also are a common motif, probably doves, which were associated with the Mother-goddess, as were also the serpents. This goddess herself may be represented in the nude or peeping from windows.

Receptacles in the rock or in pottery would naturally be required for the blood of sacrifice and for water for purification, and for imitative rites to secure rain. This we may conclude from the great bronze 'sea' and lavers, or wheeled basins, in Solomon's temple. A miniature example from the Late Bronze Age is a tripod with a circular top surrounded by pendant pomegranates, which was found with a deposit of sacred property at Ras Shamra. Plate 31

The shrine proper was surrounded by apartments for temple personnel and equipment and, as the probable emendment of the text of I Samuel 1, 9 suggests, there were apartments where the various worshipping groups ate their share of the common sacrifice, for the cooking of which there were appropriate quarters and utensils. This important religious practice is specifically mentioned in the Ras Shamra legend of the prince Aqht, where the son to be born to the king is

> One who may eat his slice in the temple of Baal,
> His portion in the temple of El.

The burial customs of the Canaanites throughout the second millennium varied according to the phases of occupation and from district to district, but agreed in the deliberate provision made for the due disposal of the dead so that he might not harm the living.

In the Early Bronze Age families and small communities were buried together in limestone caves adjacent to the settlement, which were generally artificially enlarged and finished off for this purpose. In the intermediate period between the sedentary civilization of the Early and Middle Bronze Ages (*c.* 2000), burial customs changed, the evidence from Jericho being the most illuminating. Here as at Tell el-'Ajjul and Tell ed-Duweir in the squatter communities of the period tombs were discovered on hill slopes at some distance from the settlement, a marked feature of which is individual burial, though this is not invariable. At Jericho at this time five different types of burial in contemporary tombs corroborates other evidence from the period for the occupation of the land by independent, probably tribal groups. In these tombs, which open from the foot of a vertical shaft, in one group the chamber is small, trimmed off with an adze and containing a single Plate 33 body buried in a crouched position, a male with a single bronze dagger, a woman generally with a bronze pin or a string of beads. A second type, where the tomb-chamber at the foot of the shaft is very much larger, is less carefully finished Plate 34 off. Here the distinctive feature is the disarticulation of the remains, which, the excavator Dr Kenyon feasibly suggests, may indicate the transportation of the dead nomads over some distance to a tribal burial-place. One naturally thinks of the transportation of the Hebrew patriarchs to the cave of Machpelah at Hebron or of the bones of Joseph to Shechem. Here no weapons were found, but a considerable quantity of pottery. The types, quite primitive, were unlike anything else on the site, from which it is concluded that they were *ad hoc* funerary vessels. If the burials were those of nomads, however, we should not expect the pottery in their tombs to reproduce the types in daily use at the site. Another distinctive feature of this type of burial was a pottery lamp in a niche in the wall, where the discoloration showed evidences of burning, probably part of the burial ritual, either to light the dead through his darkness or as a substitute for his life, thus prolonged till the burial and mourning rites terminated the transitional phase so dreaded by primitive society. Three other types, which vary mainly in the shape of the shaft and the size of the burial chamber, combine certain of these distinctive features, and may indicate a development of the first two types, possibly owing to the merging of various tribal groups rather than the coexistence of several distinct groups as is generally suggested.

Similar variations in burial customs with the recurrence of the same distinctive features, though with local variations, mark burials of this transitional period associated with the Amorite settlement at Tell el-ʿAjjul, Megiddo, and Gibeon (el-Jib).

With the partial revival of urban life in the first phase of the Middle Bronze Age proper (nineteenth century) new burial customs appear. Now burials are not at a distance from the settlement, but are actually in the habitable area, in some cases, as at Megiddo and Jericho, very close to the houses themselves. It has been suggested that this reflects the dread by a minority of newcomers of possible desecration. This may be true. As the pottery types found in these tombs indicate, peoples who previously inhabited the coastal cities of Syria now partially resettled certain regions in the interior occupied by Amorites. This may represent a natural expansion from congested areas invited by political consolidation among the Amorite tribesmen or the penetration of trading colonies from the coastal cities, where the power of Egypt in the XII Dynasty was earlier established. In any case the graves reflected local usage in those larger urban centres on the coast, where lack of space imposed the custom, which had the additional advantage of more adequate protection of the richer grave-deposits. Here single bronze weapons and pottery were the usual funerary deposits, and the graves were dug in the earth and lined with masonry on the long sides and closed with flat stones, as at Ras el-Ain in Palestine. A single ruined tomb of the period at Jericho was lined with mud-brick, having probably been covered in the same way, possibly with corbelled slabs. The masonry probably preserved the memory of earlier cave burials. *Fig. 24*

This type of tomb, adjacent to, and even in certain cases under, the dwelling-house is more common at such sites as Megiddo and Tell el-ʿAjjul in the second phase of the Middle Bronze Age, the Hyksos period. Some of these were used for only one burial; others were designed for the accommodation

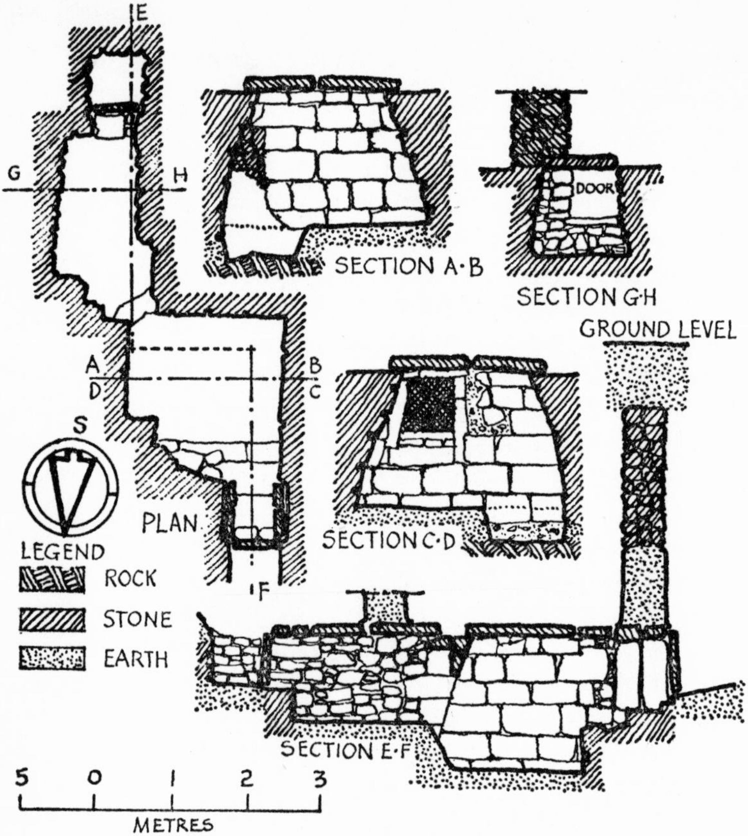

Fig. 24. Plan and section of two masonry corbelled tombs at Ras Shamra, eighteenth to seventeenth centuries (after Schaeffer)

of individuals, for whom the bones of earlier burials were cleared to one side. But multiple tombs containing about 20 skeletons, and occasionally as many as 40, were used more commonly, large tomb-chambers at the foot of vertical shafts being cut in the soft white limestone in escarpments of wadis adjacent to the settlements. The bones of earlier burials, together with their grave-deposits of vessels for food and the simpler elements of house-furniture and in certain cases weapons, were cleared somewhat unceremoniously to the back of the tomb to admit fresh burials. It is reasonable to suppose that those were family tombs, and this is probably what the Old Testament visualizes in 'lying down with' or 'being gathered to one's fathers'.

Such burial is admirably illustrated at Jericho, where apparently a local epidemic *c.* 1600 filled a number of such tombs at one stroke with their full complement of dead bodies, which thus remained undisturbed. Dr Kenyon suggests that by the same chance, after the release of gases at a certain stage of decay, the remains being undisturbed by the reopening of the tombs, certain of the contents, particularly furniture and food-offerings, were naturally preserved. The furniture, probably that of the actual dwelling-house, comprised rush mats, on which the bodies were laid, a low narrow three-legged wooden table with mutton-bones and vessels for food. Other food vessels of various sizes and baskets were disposed around the edges of the tomb. The personal adornment such as beads and ornaments, toilet-vessels and wooden combs for the women and scarab-signets for the men and bronze toggle-pins for the clothing of both indicate the care to preserve in death everything associated with the person of the living. So closely does the estate of the dead reflect that of the living that the head of the family, at least in the wealthier families, occupies the bed as distinct from others, who are disposed on rush mats, or is laid on a raised platform or dais at the end of the tomb. This type of burial, with its pathetic attempt to preserve the semblance of the estate of the living, is characteristic of the last phase of the distinctive civilization of Canaan in the Late Bronze Age.

Plate 35

Plate 37

The metropolises of Canaan were centres of international trade with purple dye from the coast and fine olive oil and wine from the country, metals from Cyprus and Anatolia, ivory and precious woods from the Upper Nile changing hands in Ugarit, and great cedar logs being shipped from Byblos. Ships of Canaanite merchants thronged the harbours of the Levant with vessels from Egypt, Crete, and the mainland of Greece, and by the end of the Late Bronze Age Ugarit at least had its Mycenaean quarter by the port. Yet the basis of the economy was agriculture, a situation reflected in the Baal-mythology of Ras Shamra, which, as we shall demonstrate, was related to the various critical phases of the agricultural year, originating in rites of imitative magic by which the peasant attempted to influence Providence by auto-suggestion.

The agricultural year began in late autumn in anticipation of the heavy rain, the 'former rain' of the Old Testament (Hebrew *yoreh*), which is expected about the end of October and in the beginning of November. When the heavy rains have softened the crust of the earth, baked hard by the heat of summer, the peasant goes forth, ploughing and sowing in one operation. Two main cereal crops were cultivated, barley and wheat, the harvest beginning with the barley in April and ending with the wheat in May or early June. The crop was reaped with the sickle and taken to the threshing-floors, where it was threshed with the sledge studded with sharp stones or metal or with toothed rollers and winnowed by being tossed up in the fresh breeze of the afternoon with flat-pronged wooden shovels, then cleaned with sieves. The grain lay on the threshing-floor protected under thorns until, along with other summer fruits, it was brought in to the storage pits by the dwellings. This is done among the modern Arab peasants with some ceremony and even with prayer. Meanwhile the vineyard was cultivated with plough or hoe after the heavy rains, and pruned between January and February. When the fruit was maturing the families lived in light shelters in the vineyard often in or on top of a drystone tower, which had been gradually built out of the stones from the cultivation of the plot (Isa. 5.2). This season was a good opportunity to maintain the terrace walls with such stones against erosion of soil. Figs having been gathered and split open and dried in the sun, the grapes were gathered and trodden out in the rock-hewn pits arranged in pairs so that the juice ran from the press to the vat. The final ingathering of summer fruit and of the grain from the threshing-floor to permanent storage marked the climax of the peasant's year, when the harvest festival was celebrated, marked by rejoicing, not to say licence, and also by the anticipation of the coming of the vital rains, the province of Baal-Hadad, and of the due succession of the seasons throughout the year. The peasant's year in Palestine is outlined in an inscription on a limestone plaque from Gezer from about the time of Solomon (tenth century), which may be translated:

Two months of ingathering;
Two months of sowing;
Two months of late sowing;
A month of hoeing up of flax;
A month of barley-harvest;
A month of harvest, then festivity;
Two months of vinedressing;
A month of (gathering) of summer fruit.

From Egyptian tomb-paintings and sculpture we know that the upper classes in Canaan wore long robes secured at the middle by a girdle, while the poorer classes wore a short robe or kilt, which was also worn by warriors. The head was usually covered with a head-cloth secured by a band, like the head-cloth of the modern Bedouin. From the tomb-painting of the Semitic group in a Beni Hasan tomb it is apparent that sandals of open thong-work were used. This painting shows a considerable variety of bold patterns in the textiles, with equally striking colours. Perforated loomweights in stone and clay from various archaeological stations indicate local industry

Plate 36

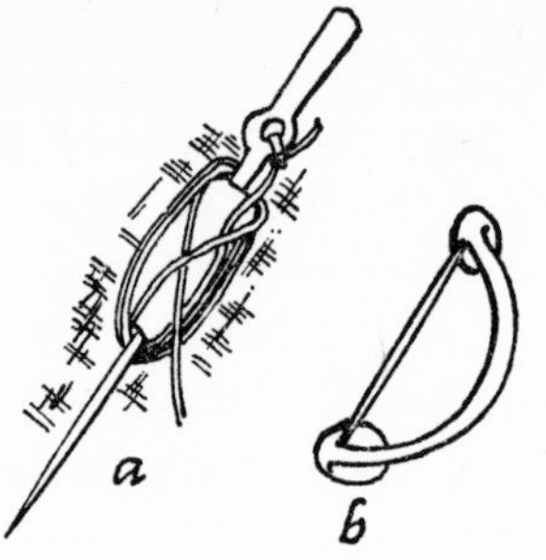

Fig. 25. a. *Toggle pin, Middle to Late Bronze Age;* b. *'safety-pin', Late Bronze Age (after Barrois)*

and we may well suppose that variety of pattern reflected the local particularism of Canaan.

The robes of both sexes, but particularly those of the women, which were not secured by a belt, were fastened generally in *Fig. 25a* the second millennium with long pins (toggle-pins), usually of bronze, perforated about a third of the length from the head, which held the two parts of the garment together by pinning and lashing with a thong passed through the hole. About the *Fig. 25b* middle of the second millennium a primitive type of safety-pin came into use, though the toggle-pin did not disappear.

The women were fond of adornment. Those in the Beni Hasan scene wear anklets, and these, like bracelets, ear-rings, nose-rings, and neck-pendants, to judge from their incidence in excavations, were as common in ancient Canaan as in the modern Near East in unsophisticated communities. Many of these objects were in gold, no doubt the dowry of the women. Then as now the husband may also have taken advantage of the traditional inviolability of women in the East to make their person the safe deposit of his capital. The ladies, however, had themselves the vanity of their kind. Like Queen Jezebel they used eye-cosmetics of antimony (*cf.* Arabic *kuhl*), which they kept in tiny pots of decorative stone, such as alabaster or serpentine, and applied with small rods of ivory, bone, or metal. They used colouring too for their faces, preparing the colour on palettes, also usually of stone, and viewed the effect

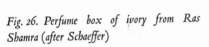

Fig. 26. Perfume box of ivory from Ras Shamra (after Schaeffer)

in mirrors, often of refined and highly polished bronze. Perfumed oil was also used, being kept often in dainty carved ivory flasks with perforated stoppers, like that from Lachish with the stopper in the form of a female head, with a spoon inserted, or like the ivory box from Ras Shamra in the form of a swimming duck. *Fig. 26*

Excellent examples of such personal adornment in gold were found at Tell el-ʿAjjul at the mouth of the Wadi Ghazzeh by Sir Flinders Petrie. Setting aside the question of the magical function of gold, the uncorrosive property of which suggested perpetual youth, we may classify these objects as decorative and functional. In the first category there are incomplete rings of gold, the ends generally tapered and overlapping, but occasionally open. These may be quite plain or ornamented with spiral pattern or granulated work, with or without pendants, which in turn may be more or less elaborate. These are rings either for the ear or nose. Much more massive penannular rings were taken by Petrie, probably correctly, as adornment for the hair. They may have formed the ladies' dowry, like the perforated coins on the hair of the peasant women among the Arabs at the present time. On the other hand they may simply have been adornment. Larger open rings in gold and silver were bracelets and anklets, still affected among the peasant women of the East as they were in Jerusalem when Isaiah had little joy of the tinkling of the anklets of the ladies about town (Isa. 3.16). Flat pectorals, generally in thin gold-plate or foil, may have been either objects of women's adornment or badges of rank worn by notables. The Pharaoh certainly used to confer this decoration on meritorious officers, as

Plate 38

autobiographical tomb-inscriptions show, and certainly very
Plate 39 handsome and much more substantial pectorals in the royal tombs of Byblos had this significance. A broad gold band,
Plate 1 hinged and clasped, was probably the diadem of the local king, like that found in the royal tomb of Ypshemu'abi of Byblos (eighteenth century).

Of functional significance are scarabs and cylinder seals mounted and hinged in heavy gold rings. These may have on occasion been worn on the finger, but are generally so clumsy that they were probably carried on a cord about the neck. They may have been seals of office, as for instance the one from the Middle Bronze Age at Tell el-ʿAjjul inscribed 'the Treasurer of the Work of the Grain', an office which recalls that of Joseph in Egypt. The purely decorative design of certain scarabs, on the other hand, suggests that they were rather amulets, which in fact the scarab was first before being used as a seal. This object, representing a scarabaeus beetle on the back, reflects the Egyptian conception of this creature. Having observed it rolling fresh balls of dung to its nest to incubate its eggs and to sustain the larvae, they connected it on a cosmic scale with the propelling of the sun's globe and its daily renewal, and hence associated it generally with regeneration. The cylinder seals of north Mesopotamian design may have been family seals of feudal barons employed by the Pharaohs of the XVIII and XIX Dynasty to rule Palestine. Eventually, however, they may have become simply amulets, the legend and design suggesting magical significance to those ignorant of their purport.

Amulets then as now were much affected. Clay figurines of the hippopotamus, cat, ape, Bes, and Horus abound in strata of the second millennium at Byblos. A necklet of gold wire
Fig. 27 from Tell el-ʿAjjul is hung with two figurines, one of the infant Horus and the other of the hippopotamus, the Egyptian god Seth, who was assimilated to the Canaanite Baal. Small

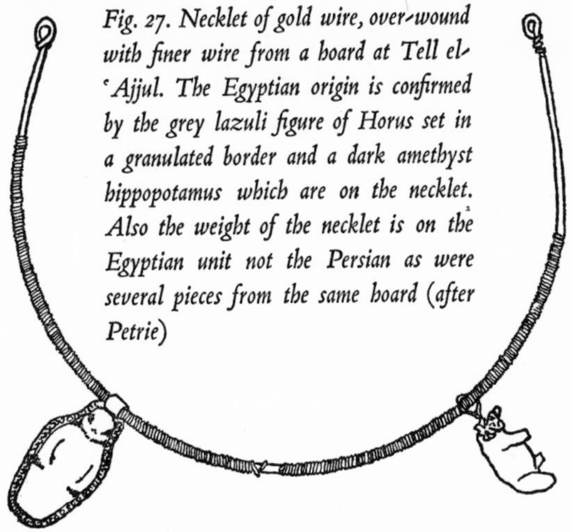

Fig. 27. Necklet of gold wire, over-wound with finer wire from a hoard at Tell el-'Ajjul. The Egyptian origin is confirmed by the grey lazuli figure of Horus set in a granulated border and a dark amethyst hippopotamus which are on the necklet. Also the weight of the necklet is on the Egyptian unit not the Persian as were several pieces from the same hoard (after Petrie)

gold flies and other insects resembling lice had probably a prophylactic value against disease, like the gold mice which were returned in the Ark by the Philistines (I Sam. 6.4), though their prevalence at Tell el-'Ajjul, the last considerable settlement in Palestine on the way to Egypt, suggests that they may possibly have been Egyptian merit awards, 'the gold of valour', to which Egyptian inscriptions refer. Quite definitely amulets are the gold plaques, usually of roughly triangular shape, depicting the nude goddess of the Canaanite fertility-cult, Ashera the Mother-goddess, Astarte, or Anat the sister and consort of Baal. The last-named goddess is probably the figure on an ovoid pendant from Bethshan (Late Bronze Age), naked and in profile with Egyptian wig and holding the Egyptian *was*-sceptre in token of her power as the giver of life and well-being. Generally, however, the goddess is indeterminate and may be one or other of the three great Canaanite fertility-goddesses. There is a general tendency too towards stylization, only the face and occasionally the coiffure, usually that of the Egyptian Hathor, being represented, together with the breasts, navel, and vulva. The use of the image, natural or

Plate 40

Plate 29

stylized, of the fertility-goddess in stone and clay is well attested throughout the Near East from the Chalcolithic period, and indicates the obsession of the subsistence farmer with the fertility of man, beast, and field. Amulets of the Canaanite fertility-goddess which the women of Canaan wore on their persons in the form of these small metal pendants or kept about the house in the form of moulded clay plaques express the age-long anxiety before the great mystery of life and birth, on which the survival of the community depended.

Bronze work, apart from axes, mainly takes the form of weapons, which naturally had pride of place when metal was locally scarce. Copper was either alloyed with tin, which with the copper may have come from Khorasan, or tempered with arsenic. But the industry was probably largely in the hands of itinerant smiths, who travelled the trunk highways of the ancient East, living a nomadic life as a caste apart, like the Qenites (lit. 'smiths') of the Old Testament or the tinker clans of the Nawwar and Suleyb among the Arabs of the present day, and having immunity among all the local tensions, like Cain (lit. Smith), whose mark was his safe-conduct (Gen. 4.15). This probably accounts for the comparative uniformity in types and techniques in metallurgy, which we note in the second millennium, especially in the very distinctive types,

Plates 42, 43
Fig. 28e

such as the handsome battle-axes, probably dress-weapons, from Ras Shamra and Bethshan in the Late Bronze Age,

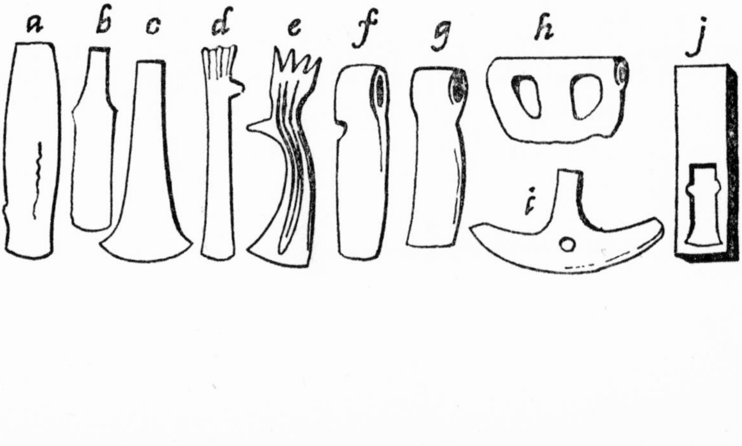

Fig. 28. The development of the axe in the second millennium B.C. (after Barrois)

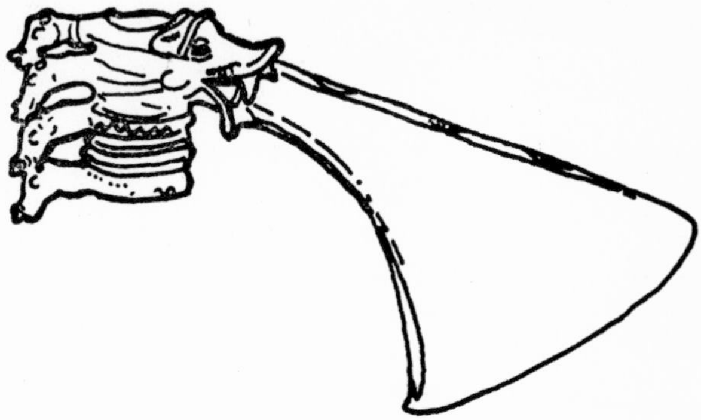

Fig. 29. Bronze socketed axe from Luristan (after Schaeffer)

which have parallels as far as Luristan. Eventually the production of the commoner types of tools and weapons was vulgarized, the articles being produced in the local city-states, as moulds in clay and limestone from various sites suggest. *Fig. 29* *Fig. 28j*

Dagger blades with fine straight ribs and channels were riveted on to handles of wood or bone, often finished in a crescent-shaped pommel of bronze or round stonework, which *Fig. 30*

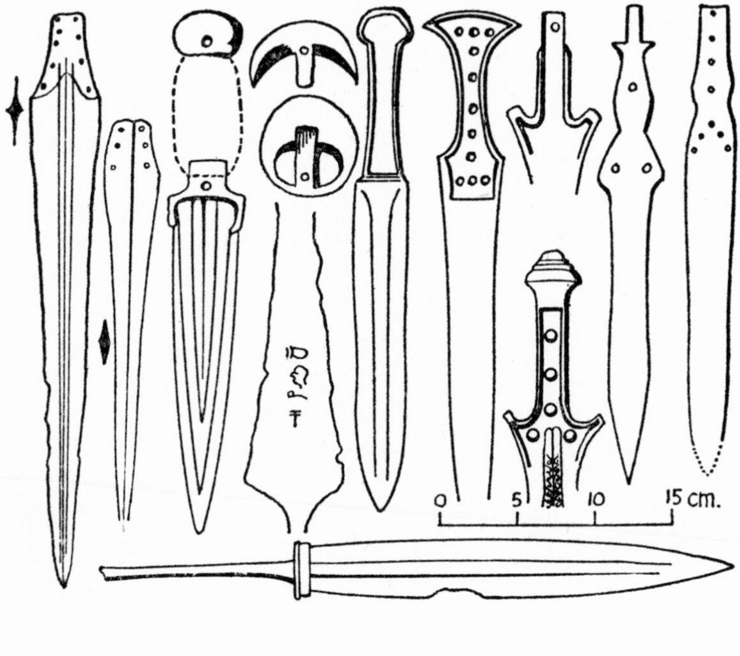

Fig. 30. Daggers and swords of the second millennium B.C. developing from riveted to tanged hilts (after Barrois)

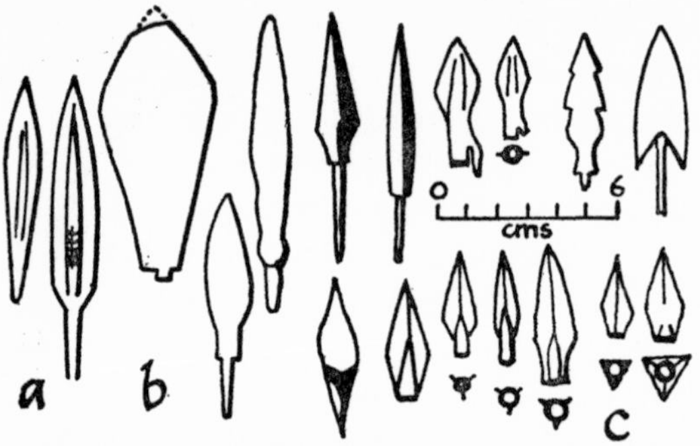

Fig. 31. Arrowheads of the second millennium B.C. (after Barrois)

must have lent great impetus to the blow. Eventually the short tang with rivet-holes was prolonged until it took the form of a long tang, which was ultimately shaped to the form of a handle, cast in one piece with the blade. This is the type established by the Late Bronze Age. Arrowheads of the Bronze Age were cast as leaf-shaped blades with two sharp edges, beautifully ribbed like the dagger blades and tanged for fitting to the shafts. Variants with three or even four edges were produced, probably for piercing breastplates of scale-armour, which is attested from Ras Shamra in the Late Bronze Age, being possibly brought westward from Anatolia by the itinerant smiths just mentioned. An arrow with a very broad head from Tell el-ʿAjjul probably served the purpose of a modern dum-dum bullet and was thought by Petrie to have been for use against chariot-horses. The chariot-warrior fought with lance, as did also the infantryman, but casting-javelins were used also by the latter. The sword of the time was the comparatively short scimitar with a narrow, sharply curved cutting edge. The handle was either short-tanged and socketed or cast in the piece with straight projection and curved blade. This was properly the sword of the Bronze Age, and is attested from Mesopotamia through Canaan to Egypt. Certain of these exhibit beautiful metal chasing on a pronounced central rib, and were either the possessions of royalty or notables.

Fig. 31

The handsome piece from the tomb of King Ypshemu'abi of Byblos, where the chased work, which includes the Egyptian royal serpent (uraeus), is inlaid with gold, may have served as a dress-weapon of royalty. Plate 41

Perhaps the most interesting development is that of the axe. The first specimens at the beginning of the second millennium
are comparatively flat blades only slightly splayed at the cutting *Fig. 28a-c*
edge. They were fixed to a split wooden handle and secured by thongs, a technique which had, surprisingly, not developed even in Egypt since the Stone Age. In the Middle Bronze Age the socketed axe appears, being almost certainly introduced
by the itinerant smiths. This, with blade either flat and full or *Fig. 28d-h*
scalloped ('fenestrated'), was still secured by lashing to the
haft, and for this purpose a small projection or notch was cast *Fig. 28d, e*
on the underside of the blade or even on both sides. It is difficult *Fig. 28j*
to tell whether plain axes were for war or peace, but they were probably tools rather than weapons, since there is no evidence in literature or sculpture of their use in war. A possible exception, however, is the very handsome splayed blade with spikes projecting behind. These are not common in Canaan, and are best known from specimens in tombs from the eighteenth to the sixteenth centuries at Ras Shamra and from a votive deposit of the reign of Amenhotep III (1411–1375) at
Bethshan. This last item is either the weapon of a foreign *Fig. 28e*
mercenary or is a trophy from some Egyptian campaign against the Hittites in Syria. The extraneous provenance of this type
of weapon is supported by the probable provenance of the Plates 42, 43
first decorative socketed axe found by Schaeffer in a building adjacent to the palace at Ras Shamra. This de luxe piece, which has a bronze socket cast around a finely tempered iron blade, and so un-Semitic a relief as the forequarters of a boar in low relief and lions' heads spewing forth the blade, with the hair and features of the animals and open flowers damascened in the bronze in hammered gold, Schaeffer attributes to Mitanni,

the kingdom in Upper Mesopotamia where, it will be remembered, a Hurrian population was ruled by an Aryan military aristocracy. This is known from the Amarna Tablets to have been an area where iron was worked in the Late Bronze Age, when as yet it was used for luxury articles, many of which were set in gold. The axe in question may have been the gift of a Mitannian king in the time when Egypt and Mitanni were competing for influence in north Syria (sixteenth–fifteenth century). The working of metals, as in the axe from Ras Shamra, may have been the product of an itinerant smith caste from the Caucasus or eastern Anatolia, as similar axes from Armenia, Kurdistan, and Luristan would suggest.

The smith's art in bronze-working on a more utilitarian plane is well illustrated in the deposit of 74 items of miscellaneous tools and weapons in the complex of the Baal-temple at Ras Shamra in the Late Bronze Age, including flat axe-heads, chisels, probably for working building stone, and adzes or mattocks with transverse sockets. Several of these are inscribed as the property of the chief priest, and so were probably reserved for work which fell into the orbit of the sacred, being thus removed by ancient convention from the profane. The other tools and weapons in the deposit had possibly the same significance, though the property mark of the chief priest may indicate a monopolistic tendency in the control of copper.

By the beginning of the second millennium the potter's art was well advanced in Canaan. The fast wheel with its turning table connected by a vertical shaft to a lower disc which was turned by the potter's foot was well established. To this wheel with its twin stone discs Jeremiah refers in his allusion to the potter working 'on the stones' (Jer. 18.3). This permitted perfection of finish, though the large storage jars and other utility types were still built up by hand, the rim only being occasionally finished off by the wheel. The potter's furnace was also in use, permitting the desired fusion of clay and tempering grits. Good examples of such ovens are that at Tell el-Far'a by Nablus at the end of the Early Bronze Age and that at Tell el-'Ajjul (*c.* 1600), the simple principles of which were a vaulted firepit with flues leading up to a chamber where heat was circulated then diffused through small holes to the upper floor, on which the pots were baked after a preliminary drying in the sun. Plate 45

The products vary in size, shape, and function, from large ovoid jars with two lugs and pointed base for the storage of cereals or oil, to small one-handled dipping-flasks. The former might hold some ten gallons and were inserted in the earth or propped up and secured to a peg in the wall by a rope through the lugs. A smaller pot with a broader, rounder base was a water-pot that the women carried on the head to and from the spring; there were also somewhat smaller jars for storing wine. Plain saucepan-shaped pots, usually decorated simply with the impress of the fingers in the wet clay, and open shallow dishes were used to contain fruit or bread or as individual plates in more elegant establishments. These were the basic forms of Canaanite crockery; they recur at the different sites with regular variations in successive phases of the Middle and Late Bronze Age.

There is, however, a greater variety of smaller vessels, ointment-pots and the like, to which it is not easy to assign a specific use. In such cases, in spite of the recurrence of regular types at the different sites, there is a decided variety, which, indeed, we might expect from local products. But one item, the very simplicity of which did not permit of individual elaboration, was the lamp. Developing from a shallow open saucer with a slight pinching together at one point of the circumference, through more pronounced pinching to the actual closing of the gap between the body of the vessel and the nozzle, the lamp is one of the surest means of dating strata in excavations in the area. In the second millennium, the

Middle Bronze Age lamp is of the open saucer type with slight narrowing at one point of the rim. In the Late Bronze Age there is a decided pinching with the resulting depression of the rim. In the more decorative types of pottery uniformity is found mainly in the Hyksos period, where a single imperial policy and a regular feudal order evened out local variations in culture and created upper orders of society with common conventions and tastes, who supplied a ready market for the more artistic products of the potters. Uniformity in ceramic types of the less utilitarian sort is further associated with extraneous cultural influence in Canaan, particularly in the Late Bronze Age, when more sophisticated Aegean types are characteristic of the period. These were mass-produced in Cyprus, the islands and the mainland of Greece in the Mycenaean age or by Mycenaean settlers on the coast of Syria and Palestine and eventually locally imitated.

Pottery is the golden key to the stratification of sites in Syria and Palestine, where dated inscriptions and conspicuous monuments are comparatively rare. Hence the wares of the various phases of our period in Canaan, as well as enabling us to reconstruct the furniture of the people, are evidence of their cultural and political contacts, as far at least as concerns the more decorative ware. Thus at the end of the third millennium and the beginning of the second, which on other grounds we have shown to be characterized in Syria and Palestine by the settlement of Amorite tribes and tribal confederacies from the north Syrian steppe and the confines of north Mesopotamia, plain, rather globular wares predominate, with affinities in north Mesopotamia. Another characteristic is a disproportionately large flat base, quite unexpected in a vessel generally globular. This ware is markedly distinct from the elegant types that characterize the urban revival associated with the establishment of the influence of Egypt in the cities of the coast in the twentieth and nineteenth centuries and the Hyksos

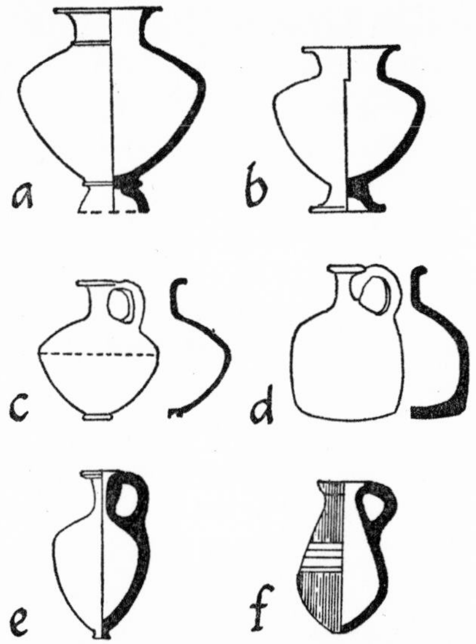

Fig. 32. Middle Bronze Age pottery types (after Barrois)

period (*c.* 1730–1580). The former period is characterized by more elegant and artistic shapes and softer curves. The bases of the large storage jars are finished in a delicately rounded point and furnished with loop-handles as against the varieties of ledge-handles which characterize the pottery of the third millennium. The smaller vessels also have soft, graceful curves with narrower bases in more pleasing harmony. Certain vessels have a relatively high foot and neck independently moulded and flaring outwards, being finished with a decided rim and ring-base, and others have a sharp carination on the shoulder, which may suggest a metal prototype. Small one-handled piriform juglets, or dippers, are a feature of the Hyksos period no less distinct from anything which preceded it, and characteristic too are the comparatively small vessels, usually juglets with double moulded single handles from shoulder to rim. The dark-grey surface, itself most distinctive, is decorated with punctured design filled with white. This decoration may be in the form of triangles or lozenges arranged in well-defined bands.

Figs. 32, 33
Fig. 33f
Fig. 32a, b
Fig. 34b
Fig. 34a, c, e

Fig. 33. Pottery of the first phase of the Middle Bronze Age, c. 2000–1750 (after Barrois)

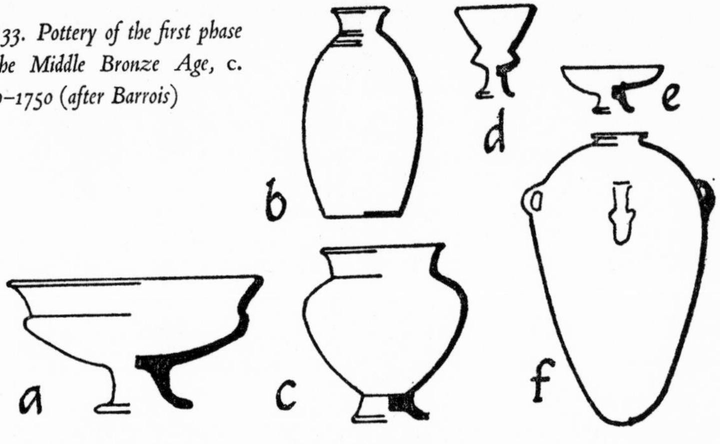

Akin to this pottery in technique, but not so widely diffused, is the anthropomorphic vase, best known from the specimen *Fig. 35* from a Hyksos context in Jericho, nicknamed 'Jericho John'. This is a striking piece with nose, beard, eyes, and eyebrows in prominent relief, and ears serving as handles. Hair and beard are represented by small punctures filled with white gypsum. From the same period come vessels of distinctively Hyksos *Fig. 36* shape with spouts fashioned as heads of animals – dog, bird, and gazelle – or with a serpent superimposed on the neck of the vessel or forming the handle. The provenance of this type

Fig. 34. Pottery of the second phase of the Middle Bronze Age, the Hyksos period, c. 1750–1580 (after Barrois)

Fig. 35. Anthropomorphic vessel of the Hyksos period from Jericho (after Barrois)

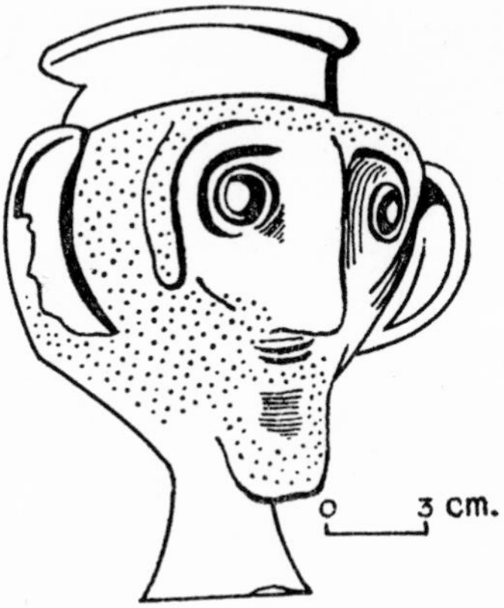

is not certainly known, and it seems most likely that these are rather the result of the individual fancy of the local potter.

These distinctive pottery types, found in conjunction with Hyksos scarabs, are distributed from Ras Shamra in north Syria to Tell el-'Ajjul, the most southerly considerable site in Palestine, and some even to the Delta. They clearly indicate

Fig. 36. Theriomorphic vessels of the Hyksos period (after Barrios)

new forces at work in Canaan, on which a cultural and political unity was now imposed. They do not, however, direct us further afield in suggesting a solution of the problem of the origin of these new forces.

A very typical pottery type which appears at the end of the Hyksos period (*c.* 1600) is the celebrated bi-chrome pottery, where the shoulder of the vessel is divided into panels and sections by broad, straight lines or bands of various shades in red or black on a pale buff ground. In these panels, bordered by chequer, crossed, or plaited designs or Union Jack patterns, *Fig. 37*

Fig. 37. Bi-chrome painted pottery of the sixteenth century, conceivably originating at Tell el-ʿAjjul, just south of Gaza (after Barrois)

Fig. 38. ʿAjjul ware (after Barrois)

various designs are painted, occasionally geometric forms such as spirals with Maltese cross, but usually various kinds of animals, oxen, gazelles, birds, and fishes. The ware is distributed from Tell el-ʿAjjul to Ras Shamra, and is found in this period in Cyprus, and to a very limited extent at Mersin, north of the Gulf of Alexandretta. So striking and novel is it that one naturally thinks of external influence. The fact is, that its incidence at sites particularly on the coast and coastal plain of Palestine such as Tell el-'Ajjul and Gezer, and at places easily accessible from these regions such as Tell ed-Duweir and Megiddo, indicates that its place of origin was south Palestine. The distribution of the ware has in fact suggested Tell el-'Ajjul, and, indeed, the prevalence of water-birds and fishes suggests a coastal site such as the marsh at the mouth of the Wadi Ghazzeh. The motifs of the gazelle and date-palm also reflect the locality of Tell el-'Ajjul with its desert hinterland and such oases as Deir el-Belah ('Monastery of Dates'). *Figs. 37, 38, 39* *Fig. 40*

Just as the presence of this ware in Cyprus and south-west Anatolia witnesses to the free circulation of trade which the

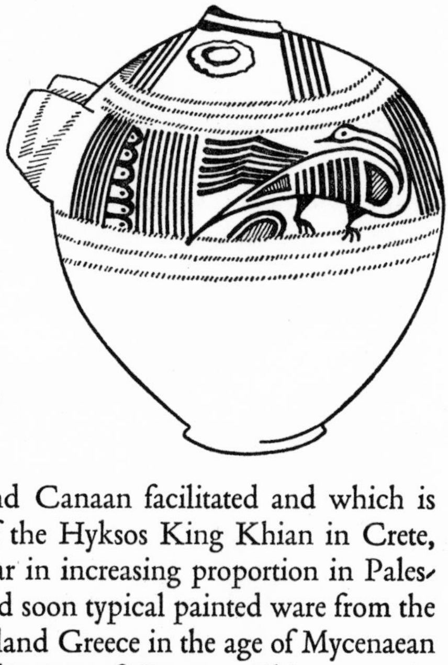

Fig. 39. 'Ajjul ware (after Barrois)

Hyksos rule in Egypt and Canaan facilitated and which is attested by the scarabs of the Hyksos King Khian in Crete, Cypriot wares now appear in increasing proportion in Palestine, Syria, and Egypt, and soon typical painted ware from the Aegean islands and mainland Greece in the age of Mycenaean supremacy floods the settlements of Canaan. This was quite definitely the result of trade, Mycenaeans frequenting the *Fig. 41a, d, e* *Fig. 5a, b*

Fig. 40. Motif of caprids and the Tree of Life on ʿAjjul ware (after Barrois)

Levantine ports and eventually living in cantonments, such as Minet el-Beida, the port quarter of Ugarit, at Ugarit itself, and at Tell Abu Hawam at the mouth of the Qishon in Palestine, where settlement dates from the fifteenth to the twelfth century. Soon these wares were distributed from the coast throughout the country, both Cypriot and Mycenaean wares being found as far east as Qatna about ten miles north-east of Homs on the upper Orontes and even in a tomb at Madaba on the Moabite plateau.

Fig. 41d The Cypriot pottery is easily recognizable. A long-necked one-handled vessel with globular body, christened by native workmen *bilbil*, stands on a pronounced base-ring, the neck being tilted back towards the handle. A few strokes of red paint on the neck or body, usually in parallel lines horizontal or diagonal, comprise the simple decoration. Another dis-
Fig. 5c tinctive Cypriot ware is the 'milk-bowl' with single 'wish-bone'

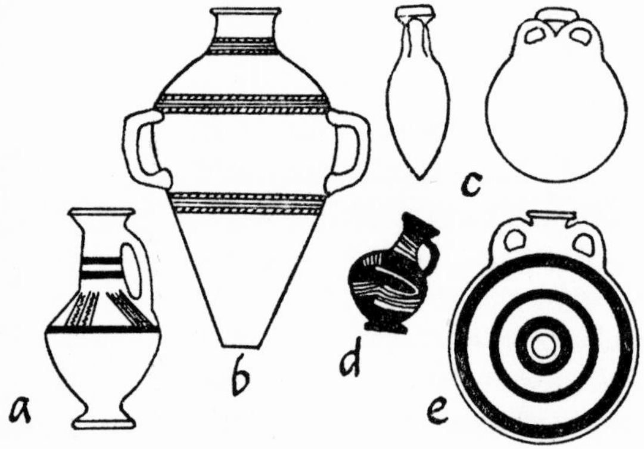

Fig. 41. Late Bronze Age pottery types, c. *1600–1200 (after Barrois)*

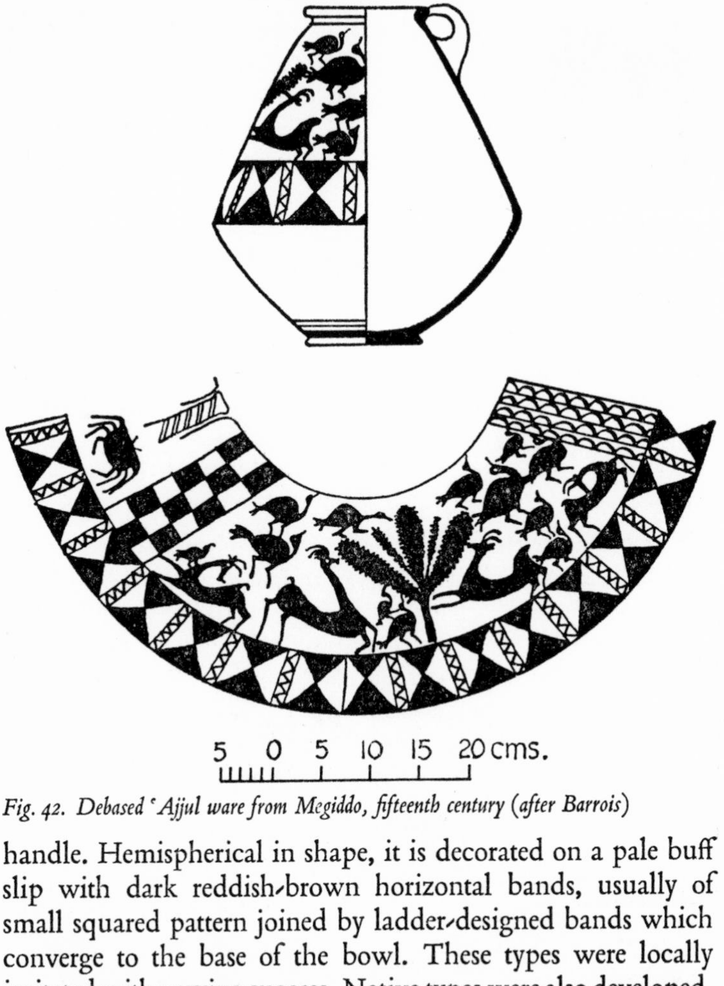

Fig. 42. Debased ʿAjjul ware from Megiddo, fifteenth century (after Barrois)

handle. Hemispherical in shape, it is decorated on a pale buff slip with dark reddish-brown horizontal bands, usually of small squared pattern joined by ladder-designed bands which converge to the base of the bowl. These types were locally imitated with varying success. Native types were also developed, such as the bi-chrome pottery and large storage jars, where the ovoid shape of the Hyksos jar is now sharply carinated at the shoulder and finished with a narrower taper towards a small flat base. The local potters now affected bolder designs, and this period marks the height of the development of technique *Fig. 41b* in Palestinian ceramics in the second millennium. In the bi-chrome pottery, however, where the motifs of birds, fishes, gazelles, and palms on panels with borders of various geometric design persist, there is now a marked stylization.

Mycenaean pottery is represented by de luxe pieces of fine texture and elegant design. The most common decoration is broad and narrow parallel bands round the vessel painted in brown or red on a pale slip. These may completely cover the vessel or be more sparingly applied. Occasionally where the shape of the vessel permits it a metope of varying breadth is left, which is decorated with painted design, in guilloches or wavy lines. The shapes are distinctive, perhaps the most so being a globular vessel with double handles converging flush *Fig. 5a* with a false spout, hence the name 'stirrup-vase', and a lateral spout.

The motifs of the Mycenaean pottery, in the debased forms *Fig. 42* which it underwent in its diffusion and local imitation through-

Fig. 43. Stylized motifs on debased ʿAjjul ware (after Barrois)

Fig. 44. Stylized motifs on debased 'Ajjul ware (after Barrois)

out the eastern Mediterranean, were combined with the geometric designs and stylized forms of the lively and original zoomorphic motifs of the bi-chrome ware of the sixteenth century. This is particularly abundant in the coastal plain of Palestine, particularly south of Jaffa, the district occupied by the Philistines from the beginning of the twelfth century; hence the term 'Philistine pottery', which, in view of the development from an earlier local type, is rather misleading. This, however, is beyond the scope of our study, since now, with the destruction of various sites, such as Tell ed-Duweir (Lachish), Tell Beit Mirsim (Qiryath Sepher or Debir,) Bethel, and Hazor, our Canaanite period comes to an end with the settlement of Israel in Palestine and of Aramaean tribal confederacies in the inland part of Syria just before the Philistine irruption. Now began the development of territorial national states in Syria and Palestine.

Figs. 43, 44

CHAPTER IV

Canaanite Society

THE STRUCTURE OF SOCIETY among the Canaanites might to a certain extent be inferred from the relative size and commodity of buildings, as Albright maintains in the case of architectural remains in the latter part of the Middle Bronze Age, concluding that the comparatively few large houses about a capacious central court in contrast to a large number of very small houses indicates a feudal order. The distribution of luxury articles in dwelling-houses and tombs might also give a clue. Here there must needs be a considerable degree of conjecture, though this has largely been reduced by the accumulation of documents. The political correspondence of Canaanite chiefs and Egyptian officers in the Amarna Tablets made its own contribution, not perhaps very explicit in itself but appreciable in the light of more recent documentary discoveries: Akkadian cuneiform tablets from Alalakh (modern Atchana), and above all texts in Akkadian and alphabetic cuneiform from the chancellery of Ugarit, supplemented by myths, and legends which relate the vicissitudes of the two ancient kings Krt and Dn'el and their families and entourage. The last are particularly important for the study of kingship and related problems among the Canaanites. The extant versions date from the fourteenth century, but a colophon to the Krt text suggests that they have been handed down with literary elaboration over a considerable period. Hence we regard those texts, referring as they do to a more primitive and heroic age, as reflecting the ancient Canaanite ideal of kingship and the social conventions of an earlier age, nearer the beginning of the second millennium. This is corroborated when we study factual administrative texts from the palace at Ugarit from the fourteenth and thirteenth centuries, where many of the functions discharged by the king in person in the legends devolved upon professional specialists. By developing the distinction between the legends and the administrative texts from Ras Shamra we may sketch the historical development of the central social institution in Canaan, the kingship, from its primitive ideal to its modification in actual practice at the end of the Bronze Age, from which point the study may profitably be pursued beyond the scope of the present work, notably in the study of kingship as adapted in Israel.

Among the ancient Semites there were two ideals of rule, charismatic and institutional. Characteristic of the first was the function of the Hebrew 'judge' and the Arab paramount sheikh, whose authority depended on their personal ability. The success of the Hebrew 'judge' in his spontaneous and often heroic reaction to a given crisis was taken as a token of the divine endowment (*beraka*). The authority of such a leader might pass to a member of his family, as usually in Arab society, but was not bound to do so, and in the case of Solomon the convention of a special Divine covenant (by the oracle of Nathan, II Sam. 7.12 ff.) and of specially revealed endowment (Solomon's dream at Gibeon, I K. 3.5–15) had to be invoked to justify hereditary succession. Once probably among the Canaanites also, authority depended upon personal ability and was not bound to be transmitted to the son of a ruler. But owing to the strength of the conception of the solidarity of the family, which was held to share the blessing of any one member, and to the practical advantages held by the ruler's family, the hereditary monarchy was early established, being in fact practically contemporaneous with sedentary civilization. In this connection a passage in the Krt text is significant as reflecting at one and the same time the conception that royal power depended on personal capacity and the natural claim of the king's son to succeed. In the grievous illness of King Krt his son Ysb claims that his father had forfeited the blessing:

Thou hast let thy hands fall into error;
Thou dost not judge the case of the widow,
Nor decide the suit of the oppressed;
Sickness is as thy bedfellow,
Disease as thy concubine.
Descend from thy rule that I may be king,
From thy government that I may be enthroned.

Nevertheless this Canaanite Absalom presumes that he will succeed his father. Replenished repeatedly from the inner steppes by nomad stock with democratic tribal traditions, the Canaanites retained memories of charismatic leadership; long familiar with Egyptian ideas, they had already assimilated the conception of the special status of the king and the royal family, who moved in the orbit of the divine.

The Krt text expresses the conception that the king is the reflection of the royal authority of El, the supreme god in the Canaanite pantheon, whose 'son' and 'servant' *par excellence* he is:

Who is Krt that he should weep?
The Gracious One, the Lad of El that he should shed tears?
Is it the kingship of the Bull El his father that he demands?
Or government like the Father of Men?

In the same text he is

. . . Krt the son of El,
The offspring of the Kindly One and the Holy.

By the time the royal legends of Ugarit have taken shape, this aura of divinity has extended to the royal family. The prince, the eldest son of Krt, is one

Who sucks the milk of Atherat,
Who sucks the breasts of the Virgin Anat.

This conception is familiar in Mesopotamian and Egyptian royal ideology, and is expressed in the ivory relief from the royal bed in the palace of Ugarit. Plate 9

Standing thus in a special relationship to God, and indeed himself eventually regarded in popular belief as invested with that 'divinity that doth hedge a king', the king in ancient Canaan was regarded as the special channel of divine power and blessing to the community.

In the legend of Krt for instance we have seen how justice in the community languished with the debility of the king. The fertility of nature likewise languishes when the king is sick. The *dénouement* of the death of Prince Aqht is heralded by a great drought. The ancient Canaanite king, then, was the channel of divine blessing in nature, recalling Hesiod's note of this function of royalty, which he describes as *geras basileion* ('royal prerogative'). King Dn'el is actually described as performing certain fertility-rites in the drought ensuing upon the death of Aqht, and his stock epithet is in fact 'the dispenser of fertility' (*mt rp'e*).

Standing in especial proximity to the divine, the king was also the channel of revelation, which he received through dreams after ritual incubation, like Solomon at Gibeon (I K. 3.3–15). As in this case and that of David, whom the wise woman of Tekoa likened to 'an angel of the Lord' (II Sam. 14.20), this insight was concerned with justice, which in spite of later devolution was always peculiarly the duty and prerogative of a Semitic ruler. In the legends of Krt and Aqht the king still hears and decides cases personally. Krt's rebellious son upbraids his father:

Thou dost not judge the case of the widow
Nor decide the suit of the oppressed.

King Dn'el's resumption of normal public life is similarly described:

> He rises to sit at the entrance to the gate
> In the place of the notables who are in the public place;
> He decides the case of the widow;
> He judges the suit of the orphans.

As peculiarly in the orbit of the divine, yet representing the community, the king was particularly well qualified to bring his people into relation with their god. He was in fact the 'servant', i.e. worshipper *par excellence*, which is specifically the title of the kings of the Davidic dynasty. Thus in the Krt legend the king performs rites of desacralization, whereby the new crop was released for public use:

> He prepared corn from the grainpits,
> Wheat from the storehouse;
> He parched bread of the fifth, [i.e. barley]
> Food of the sixth month. [i.e. wheat]

The first part of the Krt text depicts the king's wooing as a military expedition led personally by the king. The military organization of the procession in our opinion reflects actual practice, where the king led the army in person, as Saul and David had done. The fighting men rallied spontaneously round Krt as the free tribesmen of Israel rallied without compulsion round the old judges.

This, then, was the ideal of kingship in ancient Canaan in the beginning of the second millennium and probably as late as *c.* 1800, when, with the introduction of the horse and war-chariot, specialist categories and ranks of professional soldiers with special exemptions and privileges came into being in a feudal system.

In the political dispatches from the Hittite capital Hattušaš (Boghazköi) and from Tell el-Amarna and the administrative texts from Alalakh (Atchana) and Ugarit in the fourteenth and thirteenth centuries the feudal system appears to be fully established in Canaan. The administrative texts from Ras Shamra in particular show that though the king was still the supreme authority in the state in military as well as civil affairs, the day of the spontaneous rally under the personal leadership of the king was over. Regular conscription was carefully provided for in support of a nucleus of feudatories of various rank, duly invested with fiefs with regular definition of duties and exemptions by direct royal authority. Field operations were now under the control of the professional soldier, a feudal commander-in-chief with the non-Semitic Hurrian title *ewir-dšar*. The administrative texts from Ras Shamra show also that by the fourteenth century the priestly authority of the king had devolved upon no less than twelve families.

Ugarit was in various respects an exceptional instance of a city-state in Canaan. The nexus of trade-routes between Mesopotamia, Anatolia, Egypt, and the Mediterranean and Aegean, she was enormously wealthy. Strategically placed in the extreme north of Syria and of vital importance in the interplay of politics between Egypt and the Hittites, she was treated with deference by both, and exploited her delicate situation by subtle diplomacy. In consequence her kings enjoyed a peculiar status among Canaanite kings under Egyptian suzerainty, and this is reflected in the palace and its archives, which are quite exceptional in Canaan in the Late Bronze Age. Further south, the revival of Egypt in the sixteenth and fifteenth centuries had resulted in closer control with consequent modification of the powers of the local kings, as the Amarna Tablets indicate. It is not clear if all the local potentates who claim to hold the country for the Pharaoh are hereditary kings or not, and we suspect from the numbers of Aryan and Hurrian names that some at least were simply Egyptian commandants. But some were certainly native kings, such as Adadnirari of Nuhašše in north Syria, who states that his grandfather had been anointed by Thothmes III. Abdi-Khipa implies that he was hereditary King of Jerusalem in his statement that

> neither my father nor my mother has set me in this place, but the mighty hand of the King has installed me.

Doubtless expediency dictated the policy of the confirmation of local kings and their families in office. But, whatever their hereditary status, the statement of Abdi-Khipa indicates that the succession of a Canaanite king was subject to confirmation by the suzerain, and that he might, like Aziru in central Syria, be deported to Egypt if he were not amenable to Egyptian policy. The effectiveness of these kings depended on the strength and resolution of the central government in Egypt, as did also that of the limiting power of Egyptian resident officers. In the neglect of the provinces under Amenhotep III and his son Akhnaten the local chiefs had much more freedom, and, chosen by Egypt for their personal influence and energy, they for the most part personally led out their retainers on private adventures against local rivals.

From the Egyptian modification of the feudal system and from its application in the administration of Saul, David, and Solomon we conclude that it was already familiar in Palestine, the Philistine feudal system under the great baronies of Ashdod, Ekron, Gath, Askalon, and Gaza being based on fiefs already established in the Hyksos period (*c.* 1730–1580), as the late Albrecht Alt suggested. We doubt, however, if it was developed on the scale indicated in the Ras Shamra archives, which we must cite further to illustrate the full development of the system in Canaan in the Late Bronze Age since these are the fullest extant texts.

These records list the subjects of Ugarit by guilds and districts rather than by families for conscription or supply of weapons and for fixed terms on public works. From deeds of conveyance from the palace archives, it is clear that the king as feudal head of the state had absolute rights to all the assets of the realm. Assignment or transference of land was his to grant, and he might impose with the land or waive at discretion burdens to the palace in money, agricultural produce, or labour of serfs and beasts of burden. He controlled overseas trade too, encouraging private enterprise by rebate of state dues in return for a share in the profits. This economic absolutism was affected by Solomon in Israel with disastrous consequences.

Like Saul in Israel (I Sam. 17.25) the Canaanite king could change the status of his subjects. King Ammistamru of Ugarit makes Adadsheni and his family equestrian feudatories (*mrynm*) and King Niqmepa of Alalakh declares that he

> has released Qabia to be a *mariannu* (equestrian feudatory). As the sons of equestrian feudatories of the city-state of Alalakh so also are Qabia and his sons in perpetuity.

The *mrynm*, already known from Egyptian inscriptions of the XVIII Dynasty as professional charioteers, are the highest in the order of feudal warriors, as appears in certain texts from Ras Shamra which assess certain families monetarily according to their professional ranking. The precise status of others in these lists such as *bdl mrynm*, *mr’um*, *mr’u skn*, *mr’u ’ebrn* and *mšrglm* is uncertain. Etymologically the first should, and probably does, mean ‘substitutes for equestrian feudatories’, and the other terms probably denote lesser degrees in the feudal order, the last probably signifying ‘armourers’.

In this state of feudal absolutism it is not easy to assess the extent to which the old tribal ethic was upheld in the legal system of Bronze Age Canaan, especially as no formal code has yet been found. Apart from evidence of certain conventions surviving from tribal society, certain decisions in favour of women in property suits in deeds, which cite the king as witness or judge, indicate that his judgement was governed by a regular legal code.

For our reconstruction of social conventions in Canaan we are fortunate to possess long literary texts such as the legends of Krt and Aqht, both royal figures with human functions and associations. Moreover the mythological texts, though the protagonists are gods, are so strongly anthropomorphic that they are a faithful reflection of social conventions of ancient Canaan. Both of course reflect primarily the heroic past in the early second millennium. But the persistence of these ideals and observances in Israelite and Arab society surely suggests that here we have fundamental principles of Semitic society which, even in the feudal absolutism of the Late Bronze Age, the king was bound to respect.

A birth was the occasion of rejoicing; it was good news (*bšrt*). It was also a period of transition when the community was considered to be particularly susceptible to supernatural influence and potential harm. Hence the ancient Canaanite community insisted on rites of separation or ritual isolation of women after childbirth (*cf.* Lev. 12). In the Ras Shamra texts which describe the downfall of Baal before certain monsters, the mother of those is bidden

> . . . take
> Thy stool, thy settle, thy swaddling-bands,
> And stoop, couch in pain,
> In the midst of the awful desert.

In another text describing the birth of the Morning and Evening Star the mothers of the gods withdraw after the birth into the desert

For seven whole years,
Yea eight seasons' circuit besides.

At the birth and even at the begetting of a child 'Skilful Women' were employed, probably to sing and improvise incantation, like the professional keeners, whom Jeremiah (9.16 ff.) terms *hakamoth* ('wise women'). At such 'periods of passage', as the anthropologist Van Gennep terms them, it was most important that the proper influences be brought to bear on the subjects by due invocation and untoward influences counteracted by incantation.

Marriage conventions are particularly well attested. The Krt legend, depicting the royal wooing as a military expedition to besiege the stronghold of the bride's father, preserves the tradition of marriage by force, which survives in the Arabic idiom of 'snatching the bride' (*khatf el-bint*), which is actually carried out with formal show of force in many Arab societies. The parley about peace-offerings in which Krt's expedition culminates probably reflects the fixing of the brideprice. On the matter of the brideprice (*mhr, mlg,* as also in Hebrew, and *trh*) and on the whole etiquette of marriage, we are explicitly informed in the mythological text which described the marriage of the Moon-god and his consort Nikkal:

The Moon, the Luminary of Heaven sends
To *Hrhb*, the Summer's King;
Give Nikkal; the Moon will pay the brideprice;
Let the Fruitful One enter his house,
And I will give her brideprice to her father,
A thousand pieces of silver, yea ten thousand of gold;
I will send gems of lapis lazuli;
I will make her fallow field into a vineyard,
The fallow fields of her love into orchards.

These overtures are met with becoming reluctance:

Then replied *Hrhb*, the Summer's King:
O Gracious One among the Gods,
Affiance thyself to Baal,
Wed the Plump Maiden, Daughter of Mist
I will introduce thee to her father Baal . . .

The suitor then presses his suit in person:

Nay but let Nikkal answer me,
Then afterwards make me thy son-in-law.

The brideprice is then paid, a communal transaction involving the bride's whole family:

The Moon paid the brideprice for Nikkal,
Her father set the beam of the balances,
Her mother set the pan of the balances,
Her brothers arranged the standard weights,
Her sisters the weights of the scales.

In our opinion this wedding of the daughter of 'the Summer's King' is very suggestive of the practice among modern Arab peasants of celebrating a wedding by preference at the end of harvest. The wedding ceremonies too, which involve the whole community, begin at sunset. They are therefore particularly associated with the moon, which in the incantation of the Palestinian Arab is the prototype of the bridegroom, 'Our bridegroom is the light of the moon' (*'arisna dhau'l-qamar*). Thus the myth may have been used as an incantation at an actual marriage, and indeed the name of the bride appears to be used at the end of the text.

From certain deeds from the chancellery at Ugarit it is apparent that the brideprice paid to the father of the bride was given to her as a dowry. This with other personal property might be used for the joint advantage of husband and wife, but on the death of the husband or in the event of divorce, the wife recovered her property intact.

Death was another 'season of passage' involving suspense of normal activity first by the community, but in historical times by the next of kin on behalf of the community. From Israelite ritual we are familiar with rites of purification after association with the dead. David, for instance, after ritual isolation after the death of his son by Bathsheba, 'arose from the ground, and washed and anointed himself, and changed his apparel, and came into the house of the Lord and worshipped' (II Sam. 12.20). So in the Legend of Krt the king on the extinction of his family observes a period of ritual isolation, after which, in response to the divine revelation, he ends it and comes forth, washes, and resumes his public duties with an act of worship.

The safety of the community in the uneasy interim after death demanded the punctilious observance of burial and mourning rites, which are described in the Baal-myth:

> Verily Baal has fallen to the earth,
> Dead is Baal the Mighty,
> Perished is the Prince, Lord of the Earth.
> Then the Kindly One, God the Merciful,
> Comes down from his throne, he sits on the footstool,
> And from the footstool he sits on the ground.
> He lets down his turban in grief from his head;
> On his head is the dust in which he wallows.
> He tears asunder the knot of his girdle,
> He makes the mountain re-echo with his lamentation,
> And with his clamour the forest to resound.
> Cheeks and chin he rends,
> The upper part of his arm he scores;
> The chest as a garden-plot,

Even as a valley-bottom his back he lacerates.
He raises his voice and cries:
Baal is dead! What is become of the Prince the son of
  Dagon?
What of the multitudes, the followers of Baal?

From the Baal-text and also from the sculpture on the sarcophagus of King Ahiram of Byblos and from Aramaean inscriptions from Syria in the eighth century we know that food was offered to or for the dead, and installations have been found in the corbel-vaulted tombs of Ras Shamra in the Late Bronze Age to facilitate such offerings. A funeral feast completes the mourning rites for the dead Baal in the Ras Shamra texts.

In spite of the provision of food and furniture in the tomb and regular libations to the dead, the Canaanites evidently did not anticipate more beyond death than at the most an insubstantial and wholly undesirable existence, a belief shared by the Hebrews before the Exile. To the goddess Anat, who tempts him with the promise of eternal life, the Prince Aqht replies:

Fabricate not, O Virgin.
To a Hero thy lies are trash.
As for a mortal man, what does he get as his latter end?
What does a mortal man get as his inheritance?
Glaze will be poured out on my head,
Even plaster on my pate, [i.e. grey hair or baldness]
And the death of all men will I die,
Yea I shall surely die.

The same text defines filial duties, and especially those of a son and successor of the king. He must maintain the continuity of the cult of his community, on which the solidarity of the people depends, and he must perform regular funeral rites and libations to his deceased father, and with him, the founding forefather of the community. He is in fact

One who may set up the stele of his ancestral god
In the sanctuary which enshrines his forefather,
Who may pour out his liquid offering to the ground,
Even to the dust wine after him.

The king is the keystone of the community, so, in his absence or after his death, his son must take his place in the sanctuary at the communal meal (Canaanite and Hebrew *šelamim*) whereby the community is reintegrated each member with another and all with their god,

Eating his slice in the temple of Baal,
His portion in the temple of El.

So much for his religious duty. Socially the king in that heroic age, like the modern Arab sheikh, has social obligations and a reputation for hospitality to sustain. So the son is

One who heaps up the platters of his company,
Driving away any who would molest his night-guest.

In that uninhibited society of ancient Canaan in enjoyment of the bounty of Providence in ancient ritual or secular conviviality the son protects his father's honour,

Holding his hand when he is drunk,
Carrying him when he is sated with wine.

Finally his duties are, probably figuratively,

Plastering his roof when it is muddy,

and

Washing his garment when it is dirty.

The last duty probably reflects the superstition that the garment, being in intimate contact with a man's person, might be used magically to work harm on him, hence could be safely entrusted only to his son.

We must emphasize that in this reconstruction of social conditions in ancient Canaan we are dealing with time-honoured customs, behaviour rather than ethics. From the emphasis on the king's duty of justice, and indeed charity, to the underprivileged and defenceless, and in the ideal of hospitality and decency in the list of filial duties just quoted, we cannot deny that the Canaanites had a social conscience. This is further indicated by the provisions made in legal texts from the palace of Ras Shamra for women, who are notoriously underprivileged in Oriental society. In the social legislation of Israel in the Book of the Covenant (Ex. 20.22–23.33) and in Deuteronomy 12–26 much Canaanite law is probably incorporated, as the late Professor Alt maintained on the basis of form-critical analysis. But in the present want of independent evidence from Canaan itself this question cannot be resolved. In the evidence we have cited, however, there is sufficient to modify the sweeping Israelite condemnation of 'the abominations of the Canaanites'.

Chapter V

Canaanite Religion

Until comparatively recently our knowledge of the religion of Canaan depended mainly on the Old Testament and Phoenician inscriptions in the pre-Christian era and the works of Lucian of Samosata (*fl.* AD 150), Philo of Byblos (*fl.* AD 160) and the patristic writer John of Damascus (sixth century AD). The worth of these is limited. The picture in the Old Testament is distorted by doctrinal interest, however just much of the censure may be; the Phoenician inscriptions are for the most part from the latter half of the first millennium BC; Lucian describes the cult only of the goddess of Hierapolis (modern Membij), and Philo, though purporting to transmit the comprehensive account of religion in the cities of the Canaanite coast by Sanchuniathon, said to have flourished 'before the Trojan period', imposes his own Epicurean interpretation on the earlier statement.

In the early part of this century the material results of archaeology were exploited to amplify the Biblical data, but this served mainly to illustrate standing-stones (*masseboth*), rock-hewn sockets where Ashera-symbols had probably stood (see Chapter III above), and temples of various plans. Figurines, more or less stylized, of Baal and the fertility-goddesses would occasionally be found, and even reliefs of the gods of Canaan on inscribed stelae, as notably at Bethshan. These, however, did not carry us much further than the inadequate documentary data; the interpretation was largely conjectural, and no positive picture could be presented which did not depend primarily on the tendentious presentation in the Old Testament.

The situation changed with the discovery of the Execration Texts at Luxor and from Saqqara, and most notably with the sensational find of the myths, legends, and ritual texts at Ras Shamra.

The former, dating from the nineteenth century, name chiefs of localities in Palestine and south Syria in transition from the nomad to the sedentary way of life. The names, being theophoric, comprising the name or title of a god and a predicate denoting his relationship to the bearer or his activity or nature, are the first full source for our knowledge of the religion of the inhabitants of Canaan. Here in the earlier texts, those from Luxor, the god is generally named by a kin-title, *'Ammu* ('paternal uncle'), *Halu* ('maternal uncle'), *'Abu* ('father'), or *'Ahu* ('brother'), indicating tribal society, where social relationships are paramount, and reflecting the various combinations of tribal units with the adoption of the gods of the stronger tribes by the weaker. In those texts none of the deities of Canaan later familiar in the fertility-cult is named, and none of the predicates indicates fertility activities. The religion of this element in the population of Canaan, the Amorites, reflects the social preoccupation of tribesmen. The god of the tribe is primarily the guardian of its social values, just as in Israel the social bias of religion was set when she was still at the tribal stage of development. It is important to realize that before the Israelite settlement in Canaan there was this social element in the religion of her predecessors, though in the state of the evidence it is not possible to determine its precise extent.

In the texts from Saqqara, about half a century after those from Luxor, a new situation has developed. In contrast to the earlier texts, which often associate several chiefs with one locality, they show that each locality has apparently one chief, indicating almost certainly political consolidation and a fuller assimilation to the sedentary life of Canaan. Now significantly for the first time the theophoric names are compounded with the name of a deity familiar in the fertility-cult of Canaan, Hadad, known from the Ras Shamra texts as the

Canaanite Baal ('Lord'). As we now know from Amorite texts from Mesopotamia and from the Ras Shamra texts, Hadad was primarily the god of winter storm and rain, and as such, it appears from the predicates in the theophoric names in the Execration Texts, he was regarded by the Amorites in Canaan at the end of the nineteenth century. It was only after the complete assimilation to the sedentary life that he was identified secondarily with the vegetation that he stimulated.

With the Ras Shamra texts the religion of Canaan is illuminated beyond the utmost expectations of earlier scholars. Here the evidence is fourfold. In the literary legends, where the heroes are human, their religion is naturally reflected. Personal names in administrative texts, to a large extent theophoric, have a similar significance to those in the Execration Texts. Offering-lists and other ritual texts attest the many gods worshipped and offerings made. Finally the myths give insight into the principles of the fertility-cult.

El ('god') was the senior god of the Canaanite pantheon, the final authority in all affairs human and divine. His stock titles, 'the Father of Men' (*'ab 'adm*) and 'the Kindly, the Merciful' (*ltpn 'el dp'ed*), probably denote his supreme moral authority. He is also termed 'the Bull' (*tr*), probably signifying his strength. As such it may be he who is represented on a stele from Ras Shamra with widespread bull's horns, depicted seated instead of standing as an active warrior like Baal. He is also termed 'the Creator of Created Things' (*bny bnwt*). His is the prerogative of kingship, and the myths depict him as sitting in royal estate in a remote region 'at the confluence of the two streams' (*mbk nhrm*), i.e. the common source where the upper and lower waters of the ancient Near Eastern cosmology meet and mingle. El is the Canaanite conception of the Majesty and Omnipotence of God beyond the menace of any evil power.

Fig. 21

Baal, on the other hand, the most active god in the Canaanite pantheon, expresses the conception of the power of God ever actively engaged in conflict with the powers of disorder and emerging triumphant. Baal is young and vigorous, his stock epithet being 'the Mighty' (*'al'eyn*) or 'Mightiest of Heroes' (*'al'eyn qrdm*) or 'the Prince' (*zbl*, hence Baal-zebul, the god of Ekron in the Old Testament). His proper name Hadad refers etymologically to the crash of thunder with the winter rain, the manifestation *par excellence* of Baal in his power. Only secondarily was he manifested in the vegetation promoted by the rain, like Mesopotamian Tammuz, Egyptian Osiris, and later Syrian Adonis. He is depicted as a young warrior striding out in a short kilt armed with a battle-axe and lightning-spear, his helmet garnished with the horns of a bull, possibly symbolizing his fertilizing power. Baal is properly a title, originally denoting perhaps the locality associated with the god or the sphere of his activity, later signifying 'the lord' *par excellence* of the fertility-cult of Canaan. A trace of the local significance of the title survives in the name Baal-Saphon, Saphon, which means eventually 'North' in Hebrew, being Mount Kasios of the Greek geographers, modern Jebel el-Aqra, which dominates the northern horizon of Ras Shamra. This was the especial seat of Baal and the 'divine assembly', a Canaanite Olympus; but the cult of Baal was general throughout Canaan.

Plate 28
Figs. 22, 23

Baal is termed in the mythological texts 'the son of Dagon'. The latter, who had a temple at Ras Shamra adjacent to that of Baal, and is known through theophoric names and offering-lists and two votive inscriptions, was the god of vegetation, specifically of corn, which his name signifies. This association with the corn explains Baal's title 'the son of Dagon'. The theophoric name Dagantakala in the Amarna Tablets and the place-name Beth-Dagon some ten miles east of Jaffa, and his cult at Ashdod in the Philistine period (I Sam. 5.1–2) indicates his worship in the corn-bearing coastal plain of Palestine.

Reshef is also a regular recipient of offerings. He appears directly in the mythological texts from Ras Shamra only once in a hopelessly fragmentary text, and he is mentioned in an omen text as an astral deity, the porter of the Sun-goddess. He is one of the Canaanite deities whose cult penetrated to Lower Egypt in the XVIII and XIX Dynasties, and he is depicted in Egyptian sculpture as an active warrior-god like Baal, but with gazelle-horns on his helmet. This feature may indicate an association with the desert, always feared as the source of harm in the sedentary world of the ancient East, for Reshef, like Nergal in Mesopotamia, was the god who destroyed men in mass by war or plague. We believe that the gazelle-horns on the helmet of the god 'Mekal' ('Annihilator') of Bethshan identify him as Reshef, who was particularly virulent in the malarial region of Bethshan. His cult in Palestine is further indicated by the place-name Arsuf, Rašpunna of the Assyrian annals of the eighth century, on the coast just north of Jaffa. The nature of Reshef is further indicated by his assimilation to Apollo, whose shafts dealt plague, and Rašpunna was in fact named Apollonia in Greek and Roman times. Like Apollo 'the Far-darter', Reshef was termed in one fragmentary text from Ras Shamra 'lord of the arrow'.

Plate 19

Fig. 8

Another deity with similar powers was Horon, not known in the offering-lists, but invoked in the Krt legend by Krt in a curse on his presumptuous son. The god was also known to the Amorites in the Execration Texts from Luxor, as the name Horon-'abi ('Horon is my Father') indicates, and from the place-name Beth-Horon ('the shrine of Horon') in Palestine.

The offering-lists mention also the fertility-goddesses Anat and Ashera, the significance of whom will emerge from our study of the myth of the fertility-cult. The worship of the latter is frequently mentioned in the Old Testament, and she may be the goddess known from the early third millennium as 'the Lady of Byblos', and is possibly the goddess depicted naked up-

Plate 20 on a lion in Egyptian sculpture from the XVIII or XIX Dynasty, where she is named *Qodshu*, possibly meaning 'the sacred prostitute' *par excellence*. The lion is usually associated with Astarte or Anat. The fertility functions of all three goddesses being alike, however, confusion may have occurred especially in this foreign representation. Anat is represented on a stele from Bethshan, where she is named in Egyptian hieroglyphics 'Antit Queen of Heaven and Mistress of all the gods'. Both goddesses, usually nude and with sexual organs emphasized, were represented on moulded clay plaques, which are an archaeological commonplace in Canaan, Anat usually being depicted with the coiffure of the Egyptian cow-goddess Hathor. These figures were probably amulets to promote childbirth. The cults of those goddesses penetrated to Lower Egypt, where Anat was specially adored under Ramses II as a warrior-goddess, in which role she appears in the Ras Shamra texts. Astarte, so well known from the Old Testament and from Phoenician inscriptions from the first millennium, is seldom mentioned in the Ras Shamra texts, a reflection, no doubt of the local situation. She is represented with Baal, however, and actually named in Egyptian hieroglyphics on a seal from Bethel dated *c.* 1300. There is no doubt that many of the clay plaques of the nude goddess found in Palestine and Syria represent Astarte.

Plate 30

Fig. 45

Fig. 45. Impression of a cylinder seal from Bethel, c. *1300, with the goddess Astarte named in the hieroglyphic inscription (after Albright)*

The Venus-star, Ishtar in Mesopotamian religion, may have been worshipped as Athtar, who makes a fleeting appearance in the fertility-myth as a foil to the power of Baal. This may be the deity who was venerated under the title *Malik* ('the King') in the theophoric names Abimilki and Milkilu in the Amarna Tablets. He is possibly also identified with the gods of Dawn (Shahar) and the Completion of Day (Shalem), whose birth is described in one of the Ras Shamra texts, but only Shalem appears in the offering-lists from Ras Shamra. Shahar, however, is named in one of the theophoric names in the Execration Texts from Saqqara. Shalem was certainly worshipped in Palestine, his name surviving in Jerusalem (probably *warawa šalem*, 'Shalem has founded').

The worship of the Moon (*yerah*) and his consort Nikkal (Mesopotamian Nin-gal) and the Sun-goddess (Shepesh) is attested at Ras Shamra both in mythological texts and in offering-lists. The basalt figure of a seated god adjacent to a sculpture of hands upraised to a crescent and disc in the Late Bronze Age temple at Hazor probably depicts the Moon-god. Plate 26

Theophoric names from the Late Bronze Age in Canaan and the offering-lists from Ras Shamra attest many more deities both Semitic and non-Semitic, especially at Ras Shamra, where various peoples and cultures met and mingled. But the predominant cult was the fertility-cult, where the protagonists were Baal and Anat, with El as the final authority in nature and in human affairs.

The gods were served regularly with offerings of sheep and cattle of various sizes and ages, sometimes offered as holocausts exclusively devoted to the god (*šrp*) and on occasions being used as communion-offerings (*šlmm*), the blood being shed, and the vital organs and the fat surrounding them, burnt as offerings to the god, and the rest divided among the worshippers. Thus by partaking of the same animal, society was reintegrated, member with member and all with the god. Both types of sacrifice are found in Israel throughout her history. Vows also were made and paid among the Canaanites as in Israel, though there is no indication of human sacrifice in this connection as in the case of Jephthah's daughter and among the Phoenicians of the Iron Age.

The Canaanites like the Israelites expected guidance from the supernatural. Oracles were apparently sought, as is indicated by a text from Ras Shamra which probably refers to an oracle in a ceremony at a new moon festival, and the ancient kings Krt and Dn'el seek guidance for the future in ritual incubation at the sanctuary, like Solomon at Gibeon (I K. 3). The stars, as in Mesopotamia, were thought to have an influence on human affairs, against which, however, precaution might be taken. A certain omen text states according to our admittedly tentative translation:

> During the six days of the new moon of the month Hyr, the sun setting and Reshef being her porter, let the devotees divine danger.

The liver of certain sacrificial animals was also used in divination, as in Mesopotamia and the Classical West, and clay models of livers, probably for the instruction of young augurers, are known in Canaan. Of the more direct means of
Plate 47 revelation by the mouth of inspired persons like the Hebrew prophets there is no mention in Canaanite documents except in one notable instance. In the papyrus relating the adventures of the unlucky Egyptian envoy Wenamon at Byblos *c.* 1100 the local king's attitude to Wenamon is radically changed by a word spoken in the envoy's favour by a royal retainer after a fit of ecstasy, which is analogous to the experience of Saul and the dervishes (I Sam. 10).

From the Ras Shamra texts it is obvious that the cult was a complex organization. The administrative texts from the fourteenth century list twelve priestly families and with them votaries (*qdšm*) and 'women' (*'enšt*) who, on the evidence of the Old Testament, were probably temple-prostitutes. In the same connection *šrm* were probably temple-singers, suggesting that psalmody was developed among the Canaanites, as is clearly indicated in certain passages from the Amarna letters which reflect the stereotyped phraseology of religious lyrics. Makers of vestments (*yshm*), sculptors (*pslm*), potters (*ysrm*), launderers (*kbsm*), and slaughterers (*mhsm*), in view of their association with priests, are probably also temple-officials. The same lists mention *nqdm*, probably augurers, but possibly keepers of temple-flocks (*cf. noqed* designating Mesha King of Moab in II K. 3.4). *Nsk ksp* (lit. 'silver-casters') and *mkrm* (lit. 'merchants') in the same context may be those who melted and stamped contributions to the temple treasury and business assessors (*cf. mkrm* and those who minted the silver in the temple in Jerusalem in the time of Josiah, II K. 12.7–10). The temple-administration in Mesopotamia offers an analogy, and though we should expect nothing so elaborate or extensive in the city-states of Canaan, the administrative and ritual texts from Ras Shamra suggest quite a formidable ecclesiastic establishment.

The most significant texts for our subject are the myths describing the vicissitudes of Baal. Though they have undergone literary elaboration over a considerable period, they relate to the rituals throughout the agricultural year, being originally designed, we believe, to make the significance of such rites explicit and to double their efficacy. These were in fact the effectual word as counterpart and complement to the effectual rite, both having the purpose of influencing the deity by auto-suggestion. Here we designedly limit ourselves practically to the translation and explanation of the most relevant passages in the Baal-myths to document the fertility-cult, and to the citation of certain ritual texts to indicate the rich variety of the religion of Canaan.

The general theme of the Baal-mythology is the Kingship of Baal, won in primaeval times from the power of the chaotic waters *ym, nhr* ('Sea', 'River'). This kingship Baal retains in spite of seasonal vicissitudes which he undergoes in the wilting of vegetation before the menace of drought and sterility (*mt*, which also means 'death'), to emerge finally triumphant in an ever-renewed conflict. Certain passages in the struggle with *mt* clearly reflect seasonal rituals in the peasant's year, but the kingship motif and that of the conflict of the turbulent waters, which are similarly associated in Hebrew psalms relating to the New Year (Autumnal) festival, indicate that this was the occasion also in Canaan to which the Baal-myth related. On this, the greatest seasonal crisis in Canaan, on the eve of the vital rains upon which order in nature and consequently in society depended, men sustained their faith in celebrating the victory of Baal over Sea-and-River, the victory of Cosmos over Chaos in nature, and at the same time they relieved their emotional tension by participating in the vicissitudes of Baal, anticipating the crises of the year ahead, and in his final triumph. We unfortunately do not know the rites associated with this myth, but we may reasonably infer that there was an accompanying ritual. However this may be, such was the Semitic belief in the substance and efficacy of the spoken word that the myth itself was a real experience to them of the action described. As in Greek tragedy, this experience had a cathartic value. The emotions were excited and purged; the enemies of Baal, the power of Providence in nature, were given free scope, and, having done their worst, their power was exhausted.

We may better share the anxieties and assurance of the Canaanite community by hearing the myth itself in its more vital passages.

Three fragments in alphabetic cuneiform describe how Sea-and-River tyrannizes over the gods themselves. With contumely he demands the surrender of Baal, and the gods abjectly acquiesce. Baal, however, will not submit, but emerges, like Marduk in a similar crisis in the Babylonian

New Year liturgy, as the champion of the gods. Eventually the issue between Baal and the turbulent waters comes to open conflict, with the kingship at stake, for which Baal is furnished with weapons by 'the Skilful and Percipient One' (*ktr whss*), the divine craftsman:

Then up speaks the Skilful and Percipient One.
'Have I not told thee, O Prince Baal,
Have I not repeated, O thou who mountest the clouds?
Behold, thine enemy, O Baal,
Behold, thine enemy thou shalt smite,
Behold, thou shalt subdue thine adversaries.
Thou shalt take thine eternal kingdom,
Thy sovereignty everlasting.'

The Skilful One hews out a double mace
And proclaims its name:

'Thy name is Driver,
Driver, drive Sea,
Drive Sea from his throne,
Even River from the seat of his sovereignty.
Thou shalt soar and swoop in the hand of Baal,
Even as an eagle in his fingers.
Strike the shoulders of Prince Sea,
Even the breast of River the Ruler.'

Then soars and swoops the mace in the hand of Baal,
Even as an eagle in his fingers.
It smites the shoulders of Prince Sea,
Even the breast of River the Ruler.
Sea is strong; he does not subside,
His strength is not impaired,
His dexterity fails not.

The Skilful One hews out a double mace,
And proclaims its name.

'Thy name is Expeller.
Expeller, expel Sea,
Expel Sea from his throne,
Even River from the seat of his sovereignty.
Thou shalt soar and swoop in the hand of Baal,
Even as an eagle in his fingers.
Smite the head of Prince Sea,
Between the eyes of River the Ruler,
That Sea may collapse and fall to the ground.'

Then soars and swoops the mace in the hand of Baal,
Even as an eagle in his fingers.
It smites the head of Prince Sea,
Between the eyes of River the Ruler.
Sea collapses and falls to the ground,
His strength is impaired;
His dexterity fails.
Baal drags him away and disperses him;
He annihilates River the Ruler.
Exultantly Astarte cries out:

'Scatter him, O Mighty Baal,
Scatter him, O thou who mountest the clouds,
For Prince Sea has held us captive,
He held us captive, even River the Ruler.'

Then Baal goes out,
Baal the Mighty scatters him.
And [ ] Sea to death.
'Let Baal reign!'

So far as the sequel may be reconstructed out of eight tablets and at least twice as many fragments, the original order of which is a matter of scholarly dispute, the myth in our opinion continues with a description of the fêting of Baal and the activity of his sister 'the Virgin Anat', who indulges in an orgy of slaughter, the significance of which is uncertain. The text culminates in Anat's intromitting with El, the doyen of the pantheon, to sanction the building of a 'house' (palace and/or temple) for Baal, which confirms his establishment.

The 'house' is planned and built by the divine craftsman. Now Baal is housed as a King should be, and at the summit of his power it is anticipated that

> Moreover Baal will send abundance of his rain,
> Abundance of moisture with snow,
> And he will send forth his voice in the clouds,
> His flashing to the earth in lightning. (*cf.* Job 37.3–6)

The reference here to the vital rains of late autumn and winter confirms our supposition that the myth was relevant to the Autumnal New Year festival.

The 'house' completed, Baal gives a great feast to his colleagues which is reminiscent of the lavish hecatombs at Solomon's dedication of the Temple of Jerusalem. A final rite in the building of the 'house' is the installation of a roof-shutter. This had previously been a matter of controversy between Baal and the divine craftsman, which is a literary convention to emphasize the significance of the feature. This was essential in a rite of imitative magic to induce rain, which again indicates the association of the myth with the Autumnal New Year festival:

> Let the clouds be opened with rain
> When the Skilful One opens the window.

The window is opened and Baal's thunder, which heralds the rain, ensues.

While the gods had been feasting at Baal's 'housewarming' that redoubtable god had made a round of the country, asserting his lordship over

> Eight and eighty towns, yea nine and ninety.

The myth depicts the earth quaking at the sound of his voice; the mountains rocked (*cf.* Ps. 29), and his enemies shrank back to the inmost recesses of the forests and the mountains. Baal ventures to hope that he may vanquish Mot, the destructive power of drought and sterility, his inveterate enemy. Here the vicissitudes of Baal in the vegetation he promotes and the tension of fertility and sterility in the agricultural year are anticipated:

> Forthwith Baal returns to his house.
> Shall any, whether king or no king,
> Make the earth his dominion?
> I shall indeed send a guide for the god Mot,
> A herald for the Hero, the favourite of El.
> To call Mot to his grave,
> To conceal that darling in his tomb.
> I alone am he that shall be king over the gods,
> Ruling over gods and men,
> Who shall marshal the multitudes of the earth.

Baal then sends his two messengers 'Vine and Field' with a defiant message to Mot in the underworld:

> Then indeed set face
> To the mountain of *trgzz*,
> To the mountain of *trmg*,

Even to the twin mountains which hem in the earth.
Take the mountain on your hands,
The hill on the top of your palms,
And descend to the House of the Corruption of the Earth.
And be numbered with those who go down to the underworld.
Then indeed shall ye set face
Towards his city Ruin.
Dilapidation is the throne on which he sits,
Loathsomeness of the underworld his inheritance . . .

In the fragmentary state of the text, Baal's response is not certain. He proceeds to the underworld, however, having first begotten a bull-calf by a cow, which may reflect some rite whereby a young bull is chosen as a symbol of Baal and as a guarantee of his power in the season when he is in eclipse during the heat of summer. The text resumes with an announcement of the death of Baal and the mourning of El, which we have already quoted.

The goddess Anat, the sister of Baal, seeks him over hill and dale. This seems to reflect a summer rite in the fertility-cult, like the search by Isis for the dead Osiris in Egypt, by Ishtar for Tammuz in Mesopotamia, by Demeter for Kore, and by Aphrodite for Adonis in Greek religion. This was possibly the original significance of the mourning rite of the virgins of Israel in the story of Jephthah's daughter (Judg. 11.40). Having found the corpse, Anat with the help of the Sun-goddess buries it with due mourning rites and funeral offerings, a feature of which is the funeral feast for the dead god. This practice seems to be referred to in Deuteronomy 26.14, where the Israelite peasant in presenting his tithe disclaimed having offered any of it to the dead.

After an ineffective attempt to find in Athtar, the god manifest in the Venus-star, a substitute for Baal on his vacant throne, the goddess Anat, having unsuccessfully importuned Mot for the restoration of Baal,

She seizes Mot the son of El,
With a blade she cleaves him;
With a shovel she winnows him;
With fire she parches him;
With a millstone she grinds him;
In the field she scatters him;
His remains the birds eat,
The wild creatures consume his fragments,
Remains from remains are sundered.

This clearly reflects a harvest rite, whereby the new grain was de-sacralized, or set free for common use (*cf.* the offering of the first sheaf of 'green ears of corn, dried by the fire, even corn beaten out of full ears' in Leviticus 2.14).

There seems an inconsistency in Anat's demand of Mot for the restoration of Baal when the text has already described his death and burial. This is an indication that the myth, though developed as a poem of epic style and proportions, is primarily not aesthetic but functional. It has been developed from the oral accompaniment, the 'myth' technically speaking, which accompanied ritual. Hence we do not expect strict logical accuracy. In a myth relating to the growth and decay of vegetation we are not surprised to hear of the revival of Baal:

In a dream of the Kindly One El, the Merciful,
In a vision of the Creator of Created Things,
The skies rain oil,
The wadis run with honey.
El the Kindly One, the Merciful rejoices,
His feet on the footstool he sets;
And he opens his throat and laughs;

He raises his voice and cries.
'I shall sit and take my ease,
And the soul shall repose in my breast,
For Baal the Mighty is alive,
For the Prince of the Earth exists.'

Baal, eventually revived, confronts his deadly enemy Mot in decisive combat 'in the seventh year'. This may simply be an epic idiom for 'eventually'. It may on the other hand refer to some septennial rite in the fertility-cult. We know that the seventh year had a ritual significance in ancient Israel, when the land was left fallow (Ex. 23.10; Lev. 25.3–7). The conception was apparently that, in the many hazards of Near Eastern agriculture, if drought, sterility or the like did not occur in six years it was overdue, therefore a famine was staged in the seventh year, during which the power of sterility was given free range so that it might be exhausted for the following period. Possibly the Canaanites sought to exhaust the power of sterility (Mot) by a periodic 'showdown' such as is described in the sequel in the Baal-myth:

They glare at each other like glowing coals;
Mot is strong, Baal is strong;
They thrust at each other like wild oxen;
Mot is strong, Baal is strong;
They bite like serpents;
Mot is strong, Baal is strong;
They kick like stallions;
Mot is down, Baal is down on top of him.

In the tensions of the agricultural year through which they lived the Canaanites like other peasants under the same climatic conditions in the Near East were emotionally involved. Participating as they did sympathetically in Baal's trials and triumph, they demanded expression and relief for their emotions. Here was the essence of drama, and we recollect the association of Greek drama with seasonal festivals. In Canaan there was no such sophisticated humanistic development of the myth and ritual of the fertility-cult, but the elements of drama were there. In the Baal-myth just cited the passage exhibiting Athtar as such a sorry substitute for Baal that his head does not reach to the canopy of the throne nor his feet to the footstool may have been comic relief of the emotional tension. Another much shorter text, where ritual miming is associated with myth, depicts the aged El laying aside the staff of age and the sceptre of dignity and fairly kicking over the traces with two women, whose fond husbands boast of the subsequent births in ignorance of the true paternity. The actual occasion and relevance of this text is one of the notorious problems of the Ras Shamra texts, but its relation to the life and problems of the Canaanite peasant is not in doubt, and the whole bawdy, farcical tone is just that of Greek comedy. The fertility-cult of Canaan of course had its full complement of ritual prostitutes of both sexes, *qedešim* and *qedešoth* so abominated by the Hebrew reformers.

Those myths give the impression that the Canaanites were very liberal in their religion, seeking by imitative magic in rite and myth to predispose Providence in nature. Their gods were like the Greek gods, glorified human beings, contentious, jealous, vindictive, lustful, and even, like El, lazy. Granted that this intense anthropomorphism is rather the work of the artist using his poetic licence, the fact remains that there was no moral purpose in the fertility-cult. That is not a reproach; it is a natural limitation. The Canaanites, heirs of generations of subsistence farmers, sought a regular share of the means of life from nature, consequent upon the due succession of summer and winter, day and night, sun and moisture. Nevertheless their fervent hopes and the declaration of their faith in the power of Order to prevail over Chaos, their belief in the kingship of Baal won in conflict with the unruly waters expressed in the myth of the chief seasonal festival, the Autumnal New Year, were experiences pregnant with great potential. The Hebrews, settling in Canaan, adopted the festival and ideology of the myth, and adapted it eventually to their ancestral faith under the influence of their priests and prophets, as the imagery of many passages on the subject of the kingship of God in the Prophets and Psalms indicates. From this, Israel developed the idea of kingship of God in history and the moral order as one of the fundamentals of the faith which was to sustain them in the face of oppression, internal doubt and apostasy till the kingship of God was realized in One who prevailed over Chaos and Death and made all things new.

There are certain hints of religion in its historical and ethical aspects. We have seen in the legends of Krt and Aqht that justice and charity to the destitute were among the primary obligations of the Canaanite ruler, and, while it may be conceded that this was a matter of communal custom rather than individual ethics, it cannot be gainsaid that it argued some ethical conscience in the Canaanite community. The Spring New Year festival in Babylon included rites analogous to the Hebrew Day of Atonement, when the king, temporarily stripped of his regalia, underwent humiliation before the priest, and, after a solemn negative confession, was reinvested. Two texts from Ras Shamra, unfortunately short and fragmentary, describe rituals involving the king in the month (or months) of Tishri, when the Autumnal New Year fell. Then apparently the king underwent ritual ablution, while sacrifices were made to various gods, both holocausts and communion sacrifices. The probable reference in the fragmentary opening of the text to 'forgiveness of soul' is very suggestive. Another text, about which, to be sure, there is much controversy, certainly relates to sacrifice for the sin of the king and community which is assumed to be the reason for defeat by foreign peoples. That the assumption of the necessary connection between disaster and sin was no exceptional conception in Canaan is indicated in a passage in one of the Tell el-Amarna letters, where Ribaddi of Byblos, though more sinned against than sinning, writes:

> And may the King my lord know that the gods of Byblos are angry and the bitter consequences thereof are grievous. So I have confessed my sins to the gods.

Probably a solemn fast lay behind the Ras Shamra texts and the confession of Ribaddi. In any case both passages reflect the conception common in Assyria and ancient Israel that calamity implied sin in some degree, which must be confessed and expiated. Here we see that there was another aspect of Canaanite religion which went deeper than the amoral worship of the fertility-cult and was much more akin to the historical faith of Israel expressed in Psalm 78.

We should do well to remember that the Ras Shamra texts, extensive as they are, are still but a fragment of the literature of Canaan, and a fuller documentation might reveal texts of the latter type, so poorly attested at present. This more sober, spiritual type of religion is hardly to be expected to leave such striking traces in texts and certainly none in material remains. The fertility-cult with its myths and ritual of homoeopathic magic was the very stuff of a colourful and dramatic literature. It has left also the images in stone and metal of Baal the Mighty, the warrior with the lightning-spear, and of the goddesses Ashera, Anat, and Astarte in the nude with sexual features emphasized. When all is said, however, it is probably true that in spite of other and more sober aspects of religion, what predominated in Canaan was in fact the fertility-cult relating to the recurrent seasonal crises in the agricultural year, man's efforts to enlist Providence in supplying his primary need, his daily food and the propagation of his kind.

Chapter VI

Letters and Literature

SITUATED AS THEY WERE between Mesopotamia and Egypt, it is natural that as soon as the powers there developed an imperial interest the Canaanites should have become familiar with their respective languages; indeed the Middle Kingdom papyrus of the adventures of Sinuhe in Canaan refers to the Egyptian language being spoken there. Akkadian as a Semitic language would come even more easily to the Canaanites. Familiar through the legends on cylinder seals used in Canaan and even locally imitated, the Akkadian script and language eventually became the medium of international diplomacy in Western Asia, as in the correspondence between the kings of Mari and Canaanite kings in the eighteenth and seventeenth centuries and in the Amarna Tablets. Plate 17 With the training of local scribes for such correspondence, the literature as well as the script, vocabulary, and idiom of Akkadian became familiar in Canaan. The south Mesopotamian myth of Adapa, for instance, at Tell el-Amarna almost certainly served as a scribal exercise, as sundry marks in red ink on the text indicate, and a version of the Gilgamesh epic from the same period found more recently near Megiddo has probably the same significance. Certain features again of the Ugaritic myth of the conflict of Baal and the turbulent waters suggest that in spite of the local Canaanite origin and development of this myth the Mesopotamian counterpart in the myth of Marduk's combat with Tiamat (the subterranean waters) and her monstrous allies, which was the myth of the Babylonian Spring New Year festival, was not unknown or entirely without influence on the Canaanite myth. Thus by at least the middle of the second millennium the Canaanites knew something of the literature of their neighbours and were sensible

Fig. 46. Stone fragment inscribed in pseudo-hieroglyphic script from Byblos (after Diringer)

of the advantages of scripts as the medium of communication.

Akkadian cuneiform, however, like Egyptian hieroglyphics and their hieratic stylization with involved syllabic scripts, still further complicated by ideograms and determinatives, must always have been the accomplishment of specialists. They might well serve the monopolist policies of temple-estates and city-states in Mesopotamia and of the Egyptian bureaucracy, but were ill-adapted for the business of middle-men and merchants in Canaan. Hence the practical, if pedestrian, genius of the Canaanites initiated experiments which eventually resulted in an alphabet.

In the first half of the second millennium an essay was made in a simpler script, apparently inspired by Egyptian hiero-glyphs and their hieratic stylization and possibly also by geometric signs and stylization of natural objects in local proprietary marks. This is attested in ten inscriptions from the *Figs. 46, 47* early second millennium at Byblos and from a dozen small fragments from Palestine, of which the most interesting and Plate 46 also the most intriguing is that of four signs on a dagger from the eighteenth or seventeenth century at Tell ed-Duweir. The use of 114 different signs in the Byblos inscriptions indicates that this was not yet an alphabet. So few signs do not suggest that it was a fully developed syllabic script like Egyptian hieroglyphics either. The development of certain of the signs into those of the later Semitic alphabet does indicate that it was an intermediate step. No certain solution of the problem, however, has yet been propounded, though Dunand's suggestion that it represents a stage in the evolution of the alphabet when the various words in alphabetic script had to be introduced by determinatives is feasible.

We emerge from speculation to certainty with the evolution of the alphabet, which was in current use by the end of the Late Bronze Age. Thanks to the very regular word-formations

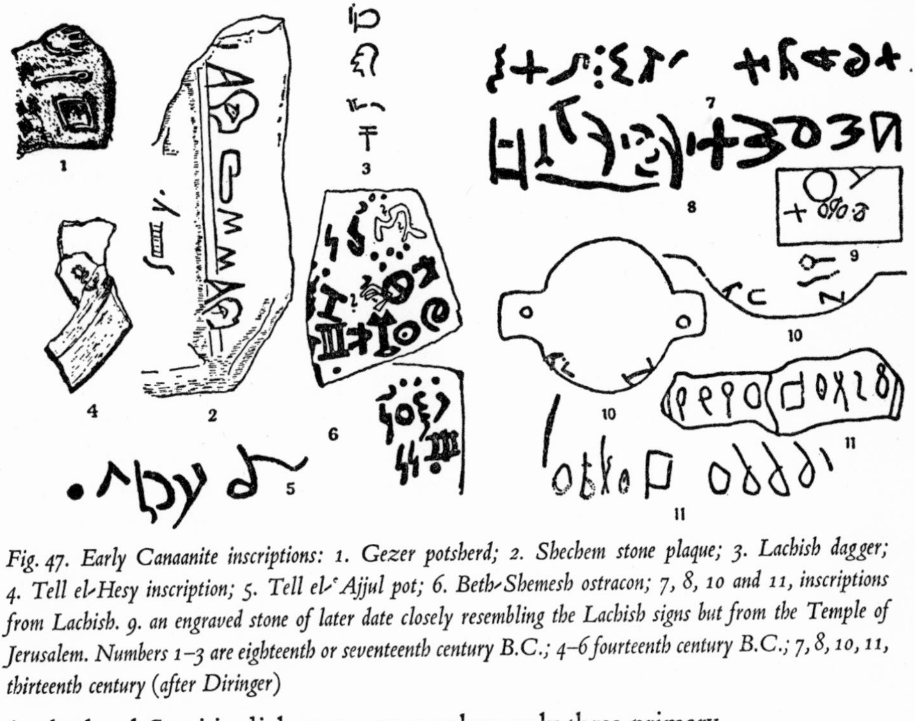

Fig. 47. Early Canaanite inscriptions: 1. Gezer potsherd; 2. Shechem stone plaque; 3. Lachish dagger; 4. Tell el-Hesy inscription; 5. Tell el-ʿAjjul pot; 6. Beth-Shemesh ostracon; 7, 8, 10 and 11, inscriptions from Lachish. 9. an engraved stone of later date closely resembling the Lachish signs but from the Temple of Jerusalem. Numbers 1–3 are eighteenth or seventeenth century B.C.; 4–6 fourteenth century B.C.; 7, 8, 10, 11, thirteenth century (after Diringer)

in the local Semitic dialect at a stage when only three primary vowels *a*, *i*, and *u* were used, vowels were considered superfluous. This eliminated at one stroke the syllabic element, which was the chief complication in the Mesopotamian and Egyptian scripts. The result was consonantal alphabets, one

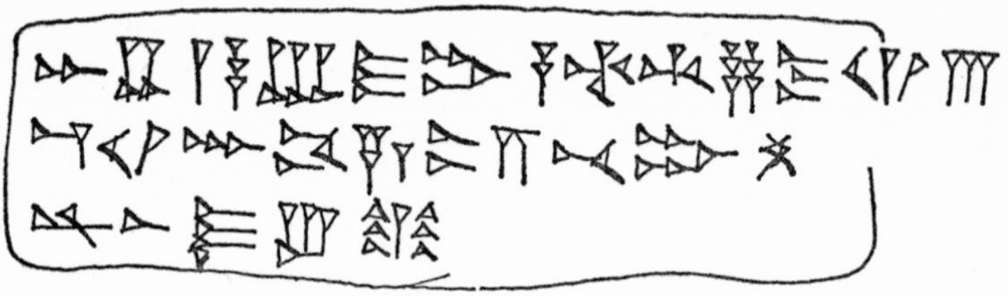

Fig. 48. Cuneiform alphabetic tablet from Ras Shamra, the oldest known ABC, fourteenth century (after Diringer)

cuneiform and the other linear. The former is best known through the Ras Shamra texts, but was also used in Palestine on the evidence of an inscribed knife-blade from Jabbul north of Bethshan, from a small fragmentary tablet from Beth-shemesh, and from a clay tablet which Dr. Paul Lapp has recently reported to the author from his excavation at Taanach. The latter, often called the 'proto-Hebraic script', is attested in its various stages of development in the Late Bronze Age from the mining region in the south of Sinai to Byblos. The former, which has three variations on the light glottal stop (*aleph*) according as it was followed by *a*, *i*, or *u*, comprises besides these three signs 27 consonants; the latter is even simpler, consisting of 22 signs without vowels. The latter, being more suitable for writing on papyrus and even for lapidary inscriptions, alone survived, but is not attested at length until historical inscriptions from the Iron Age, of which the first is that of King Mesha of Moab in the second half of the ninth century. Oddly enough nothing of this script survives from the Bronze Age beyond short inscriptions, the longest of which is that of Ahiram of Byblos, on his sarcophagus which probably dates from the thirteenth century BC.

Fig. 48

Fig. 49

Given a knowledge of the spoken tongue, this consonantal alphabet was entirely adequate for the practical purpose for which it was devised. Much better adapted than the cuneiform script for cursive writing on papyrus, leather, wood, or pottery, which was far less cumbersome than thick tablets of pre-

SINAITIC SCRIPT
DISCRIPTION OF SIGN
CANAANITE SCRIPT OF 13 th. CENT. B.C.
CANAANITE SCRIPT OF C. 1000 B.C.
SOUTH ARAB SCRIPT OF IRON AGE
MODERN HEBREW SCRIPT
PHONTIC VALUE
OX-HEAD
HOUSE
FISH
MAN PRAYING
FENCE
DOUBLE-LOOP
PALM OF HAND
"OX-GOAD"
WATER
SERPENT
EYE
THROW STICK
BLOSSOM
HUMAN HEAD
BOW
MARK OF CROSS
ʾ
b
g
d
h
w
z
ḏ
ḥ
ḫ
ṭ
y
k
l
m
n
s
ʿ
ḡ
p
ṣ
ḍ ẓ
q
r
ṯ ś
š
t

Fig. 49. The development of the linear alphabet (after Albright)

pared clay, this linear script predominated. The medium of the ledgers of the Canaanite merchant-princes, it was the script in which the annals of the kingdoms of Israel and Judah were kept and in which Baruch the friend of Jeremiah wrote down the prophet's oracles (Jer. 36). This developed into the script in which the library of the Sect of the New Covenant by the Dead Sea and all later *mss* of the Hebrew Old Testament were written. It was taken overseas by the Phoenician traders or perhaps assimilated in Canaan by Mycenaean settlers there, and adopted and adapted by the Greeks, who preserved the tradition that their letters came from the East by the agency of Cadmus. The old Italic scripts are a development from the *Fig. 49* ultimate linear alphabet of the Canaanites, who, though themselves conspicuously unoriginal, yet through their very utilitarian propensity devised the vital key to the communication of the truth which makes men free – or of propaganda which enslaves the mind.

Doubtless the records, political, historical, literary, and commercial, of Canaan in the Late Bronze Age were much more voluminous in this convenient linear script, and this is suggested in the Wenamon papyrus (*c.* 1100), which refers to the import of papyrus rolls from Egypt to Byblos and to the records of mercantile transactions on papyrus rolls to which the King of Byblos could refer. In the humid climate of the western escarpment of Syria and Palestine, however, such materials have perished, and it is the more cumbersome cuneiform texts from Ras Shamra which have survived to transmit a substantial cross-section of the literature of ancient Canaan, thanks to the durability of the clay in which they were written.

From our citations from the Baal-myth and from the legends of Krt and Aqht a fair impression may have been gathered of the nature and volume of the relics of Canaanite literature. Through lack of space these must largely suffice to illustrate this most interesting aspect of the culture of ancient Canaan.

We may give a fuller indication of the scope of this subject by a brief description of the extent of this literature and our views of its nature.

The Baal-myth occupies seven tablets inscribed on both sides in several columns. Though badly damaged in places, making the sequence uncertain, these still yield some 470 couplets of six or eight words each, so that a feasible reconstruction is possible. Such a substantial amount of text, with references to further episodes which are not elaborated in the extant texts, justifies one in speaking of a minor epic, and certainly the style is that of the epic. Frequent verbal repetition characteristic of epic is a marked feature of the Baal-myth and the legends of Krt and Aqht, and facilitates the reconstruction of fragmentary passages, further reconstruction being possible through minor fragments. Of the Krt and Aqht texts, though similarly fragmentary, we possess some 250 and 210 couplets respectively, either complete or feasibly restored through epic repetition. These are the main, though not the only, literary texts.

Those texts are all in verse, prose being attested at Ras Shamra only in certain letters, military dispatches, and legal deeds, and the conventions they use are those to a large extent familiar to us from Classical Hebrew poetry, notably the Psalms. There is no formal strophic arrangement. The text runs straight on as in the Greek epic, and the continuity is broken by the alternation of direct speech and narrative action, the intention of strophic arrangement, albeit irregular, being suggested by verbal repetition. For the same purpose the text may be punctuated by a break in the sequence of the parallel couplets, which is the regular arrangement of the texts. A tricolon where the parallelism of word and phrase is used with a climactic effect may be used. By such devices and by the use of the graphic present or the simple past tense the dramatic effect of the texts is heightened and sustained. Space does not permit a detailed analysis and illustration of the rich variety of formal conventions used by the Canaanite poets to accentuate their imagery and heighten their dramatic effect, the appreciation of which, incidentally, is very revealing when applied to Hebrew literature. It is hoped that by the citations already made and by the quotations in what follows, our rigid economy notwithstanding, a fair impression will be given of the considerable extent and character of the lively and dramatic literary texts from Ras Shamra.

The three large tablets of the Legend of King Krt begin with the rehabilitation of the royal house, which had been bereft of an heir, deal with the royal wooing and foundation of a new family and, after describing the effect on nature of a serious illness of the king, describe the king's recovery, to the disappointment of the ambitions of his son, a Canaanite Absalom. Though we do not know the extent of what has been lost, the text that has come down to us is of great value for a study of Canaanite society, especially the royal office, and in this connection we may cite the first tablet:

. . . .
The house of the King was destroyed,
The house which had seven brothers,
Yea eight sons of one mother.
Krt our sire was crushed,
Yea, Krt was stripped of his establishment.
His legitimate wife did he find,
Yea, his rightful spouse.
He married a wife and she gave him issue,
He had offspring of [one] mother.
At three years old they were perfect in health,
At four years, princes [all].
At five Reshef gathered them to himself,
At six their day was darkened,
At seven, lo! they fell down one after the other.

Krt sees his progeny,
He sees his progeny crushed,
His dwelling entirely ruined,
And lo! the whole family is perished
And in their entirety [his] heirs.
He enters his chamber, he weeps;
Repeating [his] words he sheds tears.
His tears are poured out
Even as shekels to the ground,
As pieces-of-five on the bed.
As he weeps he falls asleep,
As he sheds tears, in groaning,
Sleep wears him out and he lies down
Groaning, and he is grasped [by slumber].
And in his dreaming El comes down,
Yea, in his vision the Father of Men,
And approaches, asking Krt.
'Who is Krt that he should weep,
The Gracious One, the Lad of El, that he should shed tears?
Is it the kingship of the Bull El, his father, he demands?
Or government like the Father of Men?'

El reveals to Krt the steps which he shall take to end his mourning and win a new bride and this is carried out in a passage where the instructions of El are verbally re-echoed:

He washed himself and made himself red,
He washed his hand, his forearm,
His fingers, up to his shoulder;
He entered the shelter of the pens,
He took a lamb for sacrifice in his hand,
A kid from the enclosures,
The whole of the bread of his [ritual] seclusion.

He took a *msrr*, a bird for sacrifice,
He poured wine into a cup of silver,
Honey into a cup of gold,
Then he went up to the top of the tower,
He mounted the rampart of the wall.
He raised his hands to the sky.
He sacrificed to the Bull El, his father.
He served Baal with his sacrifice,
The son of Dagon with his food.
Krt came down from the roof,
He prepared corn from the grainpits,
Wheat from the store-house.
He parched bread of the fifth,
Food of the sixth month.
The crowd was mustered and came forth,
The élite of the fighting men mustered.
Then forth came the crowd together;
His host was abundant in freemen,
Three thousand times ten thousand,
Marching in thousands, clanking,
Yea, in tens of thousands as a dust-storm.
After two two marched,
After three all of them,
The solitary man shut up his house,
The widow hired a substitute,
The sick man was carried on his bed,
[Even] the blind man was excited.
And though the bridegroom had paid the brideprice,
He suffered his ardour to claim his wife,
Yea, to acquire his beloved.
As locusts which occupy the fields,
As hoppers the desert marches,
They go a day, a second [day];
After that, with the sun on the third [day]

They reached the shrine of Atherat of Tyre,
Even [the shrine of] the Goddess of Sidon,
There Krt the Generous made a vow.
  'By the presence of Atherat of Tyre,
  Even the Goddess of Sidon,
  If I take *Hry* into my house,
  If I bring the damsel into my court,
  Two-[thirds] of her will I give in silver,
  Yea, a third in gold.'
They went a day, a second day,
A third, a fourth day,
He reached *'udm* the Great,
Even *'udm* abundant in water;
They abode; they were at ease at the city,
They held council at the town.
The woodcutting women rushed from the open country,
Likewise those who congregated in the thoroughfares,
The water-drawing women rushed from the well,
Even from the spring those who filled their jars.
They tarried a day, a second [day],
A third, a fourth day,
A fifth, a sixth day,
Then with the sun on the seventh day
King *Pbl* could not sleep
For the bellowing of his bull,
For the sound of the braying of his ass,
For the lowing of his ploughing-ox,
For the howling of his starving hound. . . .

The bride's father, thus beset, makes overtures to Krt through two messengers:

Take silver and yellow metal,
Gold in token of her value,

And a henchman perpetual, three horses,
A chariot and yoke-fellows well matched.
Take, Krt, peace-offerings in peace.
Beset not *'udm* the Great,
Even *'udm* abundant in water.
'Udm is the gift of El,
The present of the Father of Men
Depart, O King, from my house,
Withdraw, O Krt, from my court.

Krt rejects this offer and states his demand:

For what purpose are silver and yellow metal to me,
Gold in token of her value,
A henchman perpetual, three horses,
A chariot with yoke-fellows well-matched?
Nay, but what I have not in my house do thou give.
Give me the damsel *Hry*,
The fair, thy first-begotten,
Whose grace is as the grace of Anat,
Whose beauty is as the beauty of Athtarat,
Whose eyeballs are as the sheen of lapis-lazuli,
Whose eyelids are as bowls of carnelian,
For in my dream El has granted,
In my vision the Father of Men,
Offspring should be born to Krt,
Even a lad to the Servant of El.

Of comparable length to the Krt text, and probably fuller, if we include certain detached fragments, is the text concerning the birth and death of Prince Aqht the son of King Dn'el. Here the gods, especially the goddess Anat, are more intimately involved in the action, to an extent which recalls the *Iliad* and *Odyssey*. Probably the text took its origin as a legend based on historical personages and their history, but was adapted as a ritual text in ceremonial where the king and his priestly entourage were involved in rites associated with the alleviation of drought and famine. Thus the text has also the function and character of myth.

We shall describe this text in some detail to indicate the nature of the task of recovering the literature of Canaan.

In what is probably the first tablet, after a break of some 15 to 20 couplets, the sojourn of King Dn'el at a shrine is described, lasting the conventional seven days and culminating in ritual incubation, whereupon Baal intercedes for him before El to take pity on his childless estate and grant him a son:

> Then on the seventh day
> Baal proffers his intercession
> For the impotence of Dn'el the Dispenser of Fertility,
> Even for the groaning of the hero, the man of *Hrnm*,
> That he has no son like his brother,
> Nor root like his kinsman:
> 'Nay but may he have a son like his brother,
> Even a root like his kinsman.
> Veiled he offers food to the gods,
> Veiled he offers drink to the holy ones;
> Then bless him, O Bull El my father,
> Grant him thy benediction, O Creator of Creation.
> And may there be a son for him in the house,
> Even a root in the midst of his palace,
> One who may set up the stele of his ancestral god
> In the sanctuary which enshrines his forefather,
> Who may pour out his liquid-offering to the ground,
> Even to the dust wine after him;
> Who may heap up the platters of his company,
> Who may drive away any who would molest his night-guest;

Who may hold his hand when he is drunk,
Who may carry him when he is sated with wine;
Who may eat his slice in the temple of Baal,
His portion in the temple of El;
Who may plaster his roof when it is muddy,
Who may wash his garment when it is dirty.'

With the blessing of El, Dn'el goes home, and his child is conceived, who is described in the *ipsissima verba* in which the duties of a son have already been described. In a further reassurance by El the same description is repeated verbatim. Dn'el rejoices and there follows again the identical description of the son and heir. Clearly this passage had a special significance, which in our opinion was the propagation of the social duty of son to father, which thus served in its own degree the same purpose as the propagation of the principles of the Hebrew Law in the succinct form of the ten commandments.

At this point Dn'el entertains the 'Skilful Ladies', whom we otherwise know as attendants at birth and death. Their skill probably consisted in improvising incantations, and for this purpose they were probably called to the royal bed. Expectantly, Dn'el counts the months till the birth of his son.

So far the first two columns of the first tablet are fairly fully preserved. But the last few lines of the second column and the whole of columns 3 and 4 are completely wanting. Here the actual birth and youth of Prince Aqht are almost certainly described, and no doubt the catalogue of filial duties is repeated.

The text resumes at the fifth column, introducing Dn'el discharging his public duties at the gate, when the divine craftsman, the Skilful and Percipient One, comes with a bow and arrows. The god is hospitably entertained and bestows the bow upon the young prince Aqht with injunctions to devote the first-fruits of his hunting to a god.

In column 6 this bow excites the covetousness of the goddess Anat, but Aqht will not part with it for gold or silver or for the promise of eternal life. This seals his fate, and in the first column of the second tablet Anat extorts El's sanction for the destruction of Aqht on the false charge that he has done her violence. Anat thereupon lures Aqht to a certain place on a hunting expedition, and in a fragmentary column on the reverse after a long break, is found suborning a thug Ytpn to strike him down in the guise of a vulture or hawk released by Anat – not, however, beyond the power of revival.

On the third tablet it appears from the first six fragmentary lines that the bow fell into the waters and was broken. Meanwhile the sister of Aqht, the Maid, divines from the flight of vultures that blood has been shed. In the ancient Semitic East this involved a curse upon the land (*cf.* Gen. 4.9–12), which Dn'el the sacral king, hastily rending his robe, had brought into immediate operation:

> For seven years Baal is in durance,
> Yea eight He who mounteth the Clouds,
> Without dew, without showers,
> Without upsurging of the lower deep,
> Without the drum-roll, the voice of Baal,
> For the robe of Dn'el the Dispenser of Fertility is rent,
> Even the mantle of the hero, the man of Hrnm.

The King next has his daughter saddle an ass and he makes the round of the fields, embracing and kissing such stalks as he finds in the dry land as a rite of imitative magic:

> Dn'el investigates; he goes round his parched land;
> He sees a plant in the parched land,
> A plant he sees in the scrub.
> He embraces the plant and kisses it.

'Ah me for the plant!
Would that the plant might flourish in the parched land,
That the herb might flourish in the scrub,
That the hand of the hero Aqht might gather thee in,
That it might put thee in the granary.'
He investigates it; he makes a round of his blasted land;
He sees an ear of corn in the blasted land,
An ear of corn growing in the parched land.
He embraces the ear of corn and kisses it,
'Ah me for the ear of corn!
Would that the ear of corn might grow tall in the crop,
That the herb might grow tall [ ],
That the hand of the hero Aqht might gather thee in
And put thee into the storehouse.'

Then comes the tragic *dénouement.* Two messengers announce the death of Aqht. The text continues almost unbroken into column 3, where Dn'el invokes Baal to break the wings of the vultures and bring them down so that the stricken father may recover the remains of Aqht and bury him. Eventually the tough (*sml*) old mother of the vultures is brought down:

Baal breaks the wing of *sml*,
Yea Baal breaks her pinion.
She falls at his feet,
He splits open her inwards and looks.
There is fat, there is bone.
Thereupon he takes Aqht;
He empties him out of the eagle; he weeps and buries him,
He buries him in the darkness in concealment.

Next follows Dn'el's curse upon the three localities near the scene of the murder, recalling the custom in Israel of invoking a curse upon the settlements near the scene of a homicide when the guilty party is unknown (Deut. 21.1–9);

The King curses the Source of Water:
'Out upon thee, O Source of Water,
For upon thee lies the guilt of the slaughter of Aqht the hero,
Perpetually seeking sanctuary,
Away with thee now and for ever,
Now and for every generation!'
So says he, the staff in his hand signifying finality.
He proceeds to the Myrrh-tree which emits its perfume when burned.
He lifts up his voice and cries:
'Out upon thee, O Myrrh-tree which emits its perfume when burned,
For upon thee lies the guilt of the slaughter of Aqht the hero.
May thy root never grow big in the ground;
May thy crown be brought low by the hand of him who plucks thee up.
Away with thee now and for ever,
Now and for every generation!'
[So says he], the staff in his hand signifying finality.
He proceeds to the City of Running Waters Abilum,
The city of his lordship the Moon-god.
He lifts up his voice and cries:
'Out upon thee O city Abilum,
For upon thee lies the guilt of the slaughter of Aqht the hero.
May Baal make thee blind
From now and for ever,
Now and for every generation!'
[So says he], the staff in his hand signifying finality.

So the text runs on unbroken to the fourth column, where mourning rites in the palace are described:

Dn'el reaches his house,
Dn'el lights down at his palace.
He has caused weeping women to enter his palace,
Even mourning women his court,
And [ ] men who bruise their skin.
They weep for Aqht the hero,
They shed tears for the offspring of Dn'el the Dispenser of Fertility.

From days to months,
From months to years,
Until seven years
They weep for Aqht the hero,
They shed tears for the offspring of Dn'el the Dispenser of Fertility.

After mourning comes blood-revenge, which is undertaken by Aqht's sister, the Maid:

Then up speaks the Maid, who bears water on her shoulder:
'. . . .
Bless me that with thy blessing I may go;
Grant me thy blessing that I may go with thy benediction,
That I may smite him who smote my brother,
Yea make an end of him who destroyed the offspring of my mother.'

The doughty Maid freshens herself by ablution after mourning, and, disguised as a warrior, she seeks out the assassin in his camp, where she is mistaken for Anat, who had suborned him to strike down Aqht. The text ends with the Maid giving Ytpn wine, doubtless drugged.

The text ends here at the unbroken bottom of the tablet.

There is, however, a rubric which refers back to a certain passage which shall be next read. Doubtless the vengeance of the Maid was described.

The story continues probably in one of three very fragmentary tablets, which may deal with the rehabilitation of the house of Dn'el after the death of Aqht. But this is a matter of speculation. The rubric at the end of the third column of the Aqht text certainly suggests that it was continued, but nothing more is extant.

What is missing in the Ras Shamra texts, and what might well have been expected in a repertoire which included so many religious texts, are specimens of hymns. A possible exception is a certain fragment in Akkadian cuneiform, which is possibly a hymn of praise. In the Amarna letters, however, there are certain passages which by their poetic diction and literary form re-echo passages which we have already adduced in our analysis of Canaanite poetry. These passages in the Amarna letters might well have been taken as individual examples of fulsome hyperbole, were it not for the fact that the identical language recurs in letters from various localities, some quite far apart.

Namiawaza, for instance, probably the King of the land of Ubi with its capital at Damascus, writes with an accumulation of metaphors:

> . . . thy servant,
> The dust of thy feet
> And the ground on which thou treadest,
> The seat on which thou sittest
> And the footstool of thy feet . . .

Ruçmanya of Saruna in north Palestine writes:

> . . . thy servant,
> The dust of thy feet,

The clay on which thou treadest,
The footstool of thy feet . . .

and Ammunira of Beirut uses the last figure.

In these passages we may note the poetic parallelism and the figures which reflect the cadence and diction of hymns of praise. The figure of the footstool under the feet recalls the Old Testament where it is used in Psalm 110. Namiawaza further writes, in language and cadence which calls to mind Psalm 89.36:

My lord is the sun in heaven,
And as for the rising of the sun of heaven
So thy servants wait for the coming forth of the words
From the mouth of their lord . . .

Tagi writes, in language recalling Amos 9.2:

See, as for us, my two eyes are upon thee.
Whether we rise up to heaven
Or go down to the underworld,
Our head is in thy hands . . .

and again:

I have looked here and I have looked there
But there is no brightness;
And I have looked to the King my lord
And it has become bright.
And see, I have set my face thereto
To serve the King my lord;
And a brick may slip from under its building timber,
But I shall not slip from under the feet of the King my lord.

This figure is repeated in letters from the Palestinian chiefs Addu-dani and Iahtiri.

Such passages surely indicate that psalmody was developed in Canaanite religion, and indeed this is suggested by a certain text from Ras Shamra, the first half of which refers to a number of hymns by catchlines and contains rubrics for antiphonal singing. The administrative lists also refer to singers among temple personnel.

From certain references to episodes in the Baal-text which do not appear to enter into the content of the extant text, the impression is confirmed that what we have of the Ras Shamra texts is but a fragment of Canaanite literature. The very substantial extent of what has survived, however, would suggest that the literature of Canaan was not exiguous in variety or amount. It must be remembered, moreover, that this is but the literary deposit of Canaan extant on cuneiform tablets, nothing on papyrus, which certainly encouraged more prolific production, having survived. The myths and legends of Ras Shamra and the fragments of psalms which have survived in the Amarna Tablets are of a monumental character, such as might be inscribed on clay tablets and laid up in the palace or the temple. Other matter, such as historical records and the lost work of Sanchuniathon, if there is anything in the claim that he summarized and rationalized Canaanite mythology, would be on perishable papyrus.

The permanent significance of the literature of Canaan is that it provided a literary prototype for the Hebrews. The rude invaders from the desert marches, together with their kinsmen already settled as peasants in Palestine, adopted with the new techniques of agriculture the seasonal liturgies of the Canaanite peasants. Providence in nature was enlisted in the myth of the conflict of Baal and the Turbulent Waters at the New Year festival on the eve of the winter rains. Their unique experience of God who had delivered them from Egypt and had revealed his nature and will in the Covenant enabled Israel under the guidance of her spiritual leaders to assimilate the conception of the Kingship of God won in conflict with the powers of Chaos and adapt it without prejudice, and even with advantage, to her own distinctive faith. Not for Israel the power of Providence in nature alone; the deliverance from Egypt, the Covenant, and the Law were also manifestations of the triumph of God over Chaos, and this theme was expressed in the pattern of the Canaanite New Year liturgy, serving as a theme of remembrance and the pledge of the power of God against the menace of Chaos in nature, history, and the moral order. The theme, thought-sequence, and much of the imagery and diction of the Canaanite liturgy, however, echoes regularly throughout the Old Testament in Psalms, Prophets, and Apocalyptic, both Jewish and Christian, when the Kingship of God is mentioned.

At the same time, in noting the influence of Canaanite literature on Israel, we should emphasize that Israel used this matter selectively. The theme of the Kingship of God was the only case where Hebrew religion was influenced by Canaanite thought as distinct from form. The Canaanite conception of the dying and rising god, which is expressed in the myth of the conflict of Baal and Mot, did not influence Hebrew thought. This part of Canaanite mythology served merely as a literary prototype, providing imagery which the Psalmists, Prophets, and poets in the Wisdom literature might use with as little prejudice to their distinctive faith as Milton used pagan mythology in *Paradise Lost* or the *Ode on Christ's Nativity*.

CHAPTER VII

Canaanite Art

AT THE CROSS-ROADS of ethnic, cultural, and political movements, Canaan was dominated by artistic influences from abroad to such an extent that the native contribution was practically limited to assimilation and imitation, in which, however, the Canaanites showed no little skill and a considerable degree of taste.

The Canaanites in the urban centres were familiar with Egyptian monuments and *objets d'art* throughout the second millennium. In royal tombs of the nineteenth and eighteenth centuries at Byblos, for instance, Egyptian objects are found, presents to the local kings, but there are also local imitations. A bronze scimitar, for example, of a type known from Meso- Plate 41 potamia to Egypt bears the name of its owner King Ypshemu-'abi in hieroglyphics, while another such scimitar is engraved with clumsy hieroglyphics, the name being actually written in the reverse direction. Gold and gold-leaf pectorals from the same tombs show motifs of the same inspiration, but adapted by native craftsmen. An example is the pectoral showing a Plate 39 falcon with outspread wings. This is an Egyptian motif, the falcon being the bird of Horus, of whom the Egyptians considered the Pharaoh the incarnation, but, whereas in the Egyptian prototype the bird holds the seal of the Pharaoh in each claw, the Canaanite artist omitted the seals and substituted a decorative wreath around the bird. Here typically Canaanite art is at the best a good copy of a foreign prototype with little attempt at originality.

In those tombs there is metal-work that points probably in another direction. Silver vessels with long spouts and high loop- Plate 4 handle like a modern teapot and finished with a shapely fluted body derive directly from Crete. A decorative knife

Plate 44 with silver blade damascened in gold, the handle being covered with gold foil and niello-work, may indicate a technique of Anatolian metal-workers, as is suggested by inlay of gold and silver on copper in the figurines of two deities with Anatolian, probably Hurrian, affinities from Ras Shamra *c.* nineteenth to Plates 49, 50 seventeenth centuries. Cruder bronze figurines similarly grooved for inlay were among the foundation-deposits from the temple of the Lady of Byblos which was rebuilt *c.* 2000.

Other foundation-deposits from Byblos at this time include cylinder-seals, once used for sealing stoppers in jars of agricultural produce. The cylinder-seal itself suggests Mesopotamian influence, to say nothing of the motifs, Hadad in a long robe with his lightning standing on a bull, the naked Ishtar, bull-man figures, and the guilloche design associated with Upper Mesopotamia and later distinctive in Mitannian art. The head-dress of the devotees on a certain seal with the Egyptian uraeus completes the mixture of cultural influences, but points to native execution, which is fairly accurate and well-composed, if exhibiting a certain *horror vacui*, which is probably the legacy of a north Mesopotamian prototype.

The same mixture of artistic influences of Egypt and Meso-*Fig. 21* potamia is exhibited in the relief from Ras Shamra of a god, usually identified, though on no certain grounds, with El, and a devotee. Here the hair-style and horned head-gear of the bearded god are Mesopotamian, but the worshipper wears the Egyptian head-dress with the royal uraeus. The mixture of styles indicates local work, of no distinctive merit besides. The postures of god and worshipper are conventional and the features are expressionless.

There is much more action in the sculpture of the bearded Plate 28 Baal, who strides above two registers of undulations brandishing a mace and carrying a lightning-spear. He wears a peaked head-dress ornamented with bull's horns and a warrior's short kilt with a dagger in a curved sheath. The last feature and the

Fig. 50. Sculpture of a god, Osiris (?), with foliage head-dress from Ras Shamra (after Schaeffer)

overlap of the kilt on the right leg connects the figure with the representation of the Hurrian weather-god Teshub in late Hittite art, as in the sculpture at the gate of Boghazköi. But the two registers of undulations under the figure, according to our interpretation, represent the upper waters (clouds) and the lower waters of Mesopotamian cosmology, hence the description of Baal in the Ras Shamra mythology as 'He who mounts the Clouds'. This was the prototype of the conventional representation of Baal in bronze figurines which have been found at Minet el-Beida and Tell ed-Duweir (fourteenth–thirteenth centuries). If this relief is as early as Professor Schaeffer suggests (*c.* 2000) it would coincide with the first phase of Hurrian penetration of north Syria.

Plate 48

Figs. 22, 23

Fig. 50 The curious representation in a stele from Ras Shamra of a god with the strange head-dress which has been taken as a plume, but is probably foliage, shows a mixture of Anatolian and Egyptian influences. The figure strides out in the short kilt with overlap on the right leg and a straight dagger at his girdle. He carries a plain spear with the butt resting on the ground and in the other hand a short crook. The features are indeterminate, though he appears to have a beard and a curled horn, or perhaps a pair in profile. The head in fact may be bovine or caprid rather than anthropomorphic. The Anatolian origin is suggested not only by the kilt with straight dagger but by the shoes with upturned toes, characteristic of mountaineers in the Mediterranean region till the present day. The short crook, however, is the symbol of the Egyptian Osiris, and the foliage head-dress may express the association of Osiris with the tamarisk, which had currency in the Osiris myth associated with Byblos, where the body of the dead Osiris was reputed to have been washed up and to have been transformed into a tamarisk – hence the title of Osiris 'He of the Tamarisk'. There is nothing in the sculpture which makes it artistically distinctive, and we cite it only to illustrate the multiple foreign influences on Canaanite art.

Anatolian influence is probably again present in two bronze figurines from Ras Shamra, one of a seated goddess, and the other of a free-standing god.

Plate 49 The former, of copper and 24 cm. high, has been moulded in the flat, then bent into a seated position. The body with its full-edged robe and its disproportionately long legs and short bust is of no artistic consequence. The front is moulded in the round and the back flat. The head, however, is noteworthy. Crowned by a high-peaked turban, it represents a brachycephalic Armenoid type, with prominent cheek-bones and typically pronounced high-bridged aquiline nose. The cheeks are becomingly full, the lips full and definite, and the regular rounded chin dimpled. The eye-sockets are large, but the inlay, probably of precious stones, has gone. Slightly arched grooves indicate that the eyebrows were inlayed with precious metal, and grooves at the back of the head and round the edge of the back show that the figure was plated, possibly with gold-foil on lead. The face makes a good impression of calm beauty even if there is a lack of expression, which may intentionally convey divine dignity. The Armenoid features suggest a Hurrian deity, perhaps Khipa, and no doubt if the object she once held in her left hand had survived we should have had a more definite clue to her identity. The workmanship also was probably Hurrian, the technical efficiency of the metal-work probably pointing to an origin with the metal-working peoples of Anatolia. From the same level comes the upright figure of a god about 20 cm. high also of copper and plated, except the face, with electrum. Here again only the face has any artistic merit, though inferior to the goddess. The face is broad and the skull brachycephalic. The eyes, set with light and dull stone to represent whites and pupils respectively, are less naturalistic than those of the goddess, being set in almost square sockets. The nose is less prominent, being in fact almost straight. The brow is broad and receding, the chin full and rounded, and the mouth small and drooping at the corners. This was perhaps intended to convey the impression of austerity, but it is hardly successful and suggests rather petulance. The head-dress is particularly significant. It is conical, vertically fluted or striped, and tilted forward, being exactly paralleled by the head-dress of a god in a sculpture from Yazilikaia in Asia Minor of the thirteenth century.

Plate 50

Fig. 51

The features of Baal of the lightning-spear were translated into the round in bronze figurines plaited or inlaid with gold and silver. The head of one of these from Minet el-Beida is particularly well preserved with its tall, conical helmet, but without the customary bull's horns. The regular rounded

Fig. 22

Fig. 51. Hittite sculptures from a rock-face at Yazilikaia illustrating the tilted, fluted head-dress of the bronze figurine in Plate 50 (after Akurgal)

features recall those of the seated goddess, and the type is again Armenoid. The nose is less pronounced than that of the goddess and the ears are better placed and proportioned. So naturalistic are the features that one might almost postulate an actual model. Indeed the identical features may be met with commonly in the district of Latakia today. On the other hand, the Armenoid features may have been conventionalized in the representations of the god from the time that they were introduced to Canaan by the Anatolian metal-workers in the beginning of the second millennium. These features are strik-

Plate 8

ingly reproduced in ivory in an exquisite little head, which has been taken as that of one of the kings of Ugarit in the Late Bronze Age. If this is so, it seems to us that this is less a portrait, though this is always possible, than the reproduction of the stylized features of Baal. Professor Schaeffer, following the suggestion of M. Dunand, thinks that the head is that of a female, which may be indicated by the stylized curls that protrude beneath the headgear. The nearest rivals to those heads

Fig. 52

are the features on a decorative vase finished in faience from the Mycenaean settlement at Minet el-Beida, unfortunately dam-

Fig. 52. Anthropomorphic vessel of Mycenaean design finished in glazed faience, from Minet el-Beida, fourteenth century (after Schaeffer)

aged, and the very naturalistic features tending to caricature on a bronze weight in the form of a human head, probably that of the merchant himself, from the same community, which is the *pièce de résistance* in bronze-casting in Canaan. The superiority of the features in these bronzes is probably owing to the fact that they were first modelled in the plastic medium of wax in preparation for the bipartite clay mould from which the figurines were produced by the *cire perdue* technique. Even so the superiority of those figures with their Armenoid features seems to indicate long experience in feature-moulding by Anatolian artists working with native metal-workers. *Fig. 53*

We note as significant that the copper figurines of Baal and the seated goddess are not certainly native work, and the same may be said of the magnificent stone head from the temple in Level VII (eighteenth century) at Atchana. This, with its generous naturalistic features, gives a fine impression of royal strength and dignity and is certainly the finest piece of feature-sculpture from Bronze Age Syria, but it is almost certainly the work of a foreigner. The excavator Sir Leonard Woolley attributes it to a representative of a Sumerian school of art in Plate 51

Fig. 53. Bronze weight (180 gr.) in the form of a human head, probably a portrait of the merchant and probably Mycenaean work, from Ras Shamra, fifteenth or fourteenth century (after Schaeffer)

north Mesopotamia, which has so far not been discovered. Whatever the origin may be, it is unique and can scarcely be cited as an example of Canaanite art.

Ivory-carving was apparently a speciality of the Canaanites, especially in the coastal cities. Low relief or incision on flat plaques for inlay was their speciality, probably a by-product of furniture-making, for which the fine cedar of Lebanon and Amanus was an incentive.

The earliest specimens of Canaanite ivory-work are the various objects from the palace of Ugarit at the end of the Late Bronze Age. Specially noteworthy is a decorative horn fashioned out of a whole elephant tusk; this, however, was damaged by the fire that destroyed the palace. On the inside curve a naked goddess is preserved standing between two winged sphinxes. Below a border on which the figures apparently stand there are traces of a panel of lions, probably seated, with tails intertwined, as in the lower border of the sarcophagus of King Ahiram of Byblos. Here perfect symmetry is observed.

Plates 56, 57

The sphinxes though generally stylized are naturalistically represented in forelegs and facial features. The figure of the goddess is the noteworthy feature. In spite of the disproportionately large head and the unnatural tiptoe stance the body is gracefully rendered and the face is naturalistic with an expression of calm dignity and conscious superiority befitting a goddess.

The most interesting of these ivories are the eight panels 24 cm. by 10 cm. by 12 cm. once set together in a frame of Plates 9, 10 wood and ivory with friezes above and below depicting beasts in combat and hunting scenes, the lower register being further embellished by a border of fretted ivory with representations of the sacred tree, the eye of Horus, and other motifs of an apotropaic or auspicious nature. The pieces, riveted back to back, formed the foot panel of the royal bed, Professor Schaeffer has adduced from Egyptian analogies from the Amarna period. The panels, of greater documentary than artistic value, though striking and not unpleasing in composition, depict scenes from the life of the king. Those on the inside are more intimate. Plate 9 The first depicts a goddess suckling a pair of boys or young men. She wears a long robe, two pairs of wings, Hathor coiffure with horns surmounted by a disc enclosing stylized lightning and stars, and doubtless representing Anat, the redoubtable sister of Baal the god of lightning and winter storms. The motif of suckling by the goddess is a commonplace in the ideology of kingship in ancient Mesopotamia, Egypt, and Canaan, where it is referred to in the Legend of King Krt. The twin figures, then, are royal, probably representing not two persons but one, the two being depicted for the sake of symmetry. The work as a whole lacks grace, particularly the robed body of the goddess whose feet are in profile but who is otherwise shown full on. The feet of the sucking figures, though in profile, present all five toes! The facial features of the goddess, however, are successfully executed in relief, and, if wanting in expression, certainly convey the serene dignity of deity. Another panel depicts a princess, probably the royal bride, making an offering to the goddess. Another depicts the royal pair, the queen with her left arm about the king's neck and offering him perfume with her right hand. He, as far as the fragmentary panel indicates, has his right arm about her neck while his left hand is laid gently on her breast. Enough of her abdomen is displayed to hint delicately at pregnancy. Here again there is a certain gaucherie, the king's foot showing all five toes, and the face somewhat lacking in expression. The last scene on the inner face shows a huntsman bringing game to the king. In association with these intimate scenes of the life of the royal pair we may note that there are two stylistic representations of the fertility-symbol of the tree of life. This motif befitted panels for the royal bed, and the use of ivory in panelling and independent *objets d'art* in the period was most likely prompted by the role that the substance has always played in magic to promote potency. This probably accounts for the motifs of the tree of life, the mother-goddess, the benevolent dwarf Bes, and the naked females, which recur in the Bronze Age ivories of Canaan.

Plates 16, 30

The outer face depicts scenes from the public life of the king. Most noteworthy is that of the king clutching a Semitic enemy by the hair and piercing his eye with a short stabbing sword. His Majesty in such a moment of triumph is singularly lifeless and phlegmatic, but his enemy, half-kneeling with hands raised in supplication, is full of life. The features of both, in profile, are well executed except for the disproportionately large eye, and might well serve as a portrait of a Semite of Canaan at that time.

True to their tradition, the Canaanites in their ivory-work curbed their initiative and deferred to Mesopotamian and Egyptian motifs, as in the figure of the winged, bearded genie

from Megiddo, a version of the Egyptian Bes, the grotesque Plate 16
dwarf, who was the protector of women in pregnancy, of
children, and people in sleep, and the scene of a royal triumph,
where the king's throne is supported by Mesopotamian winged *Fig. 15*
sphinxes. The life-symbol of the lotus in the king's hand is an
Egyptian motif, but all the other features are Canaanite. Here
the bodies are particularly well drawn, and the composition is
good, except for a certain *horror vacui*, which prompted the
filling of spaces with birds and three-stemmed plants. Apparently depicting the king receiving the queen, with a female
musician, and a warrior who leads in a chariot with its driver
preceded by prisoners of war in bonds, the piece probably
depicts two different scenes, the return of the king from war and
his entertainment by the queen and a female musician in
peace. In the plaque, which is a line-incision rather than a relief,
the three-stemmed flowers may be an artistic convention to
divide the scenes. The plaque of Bes in open-work shows a Plate 16
certain originality in the combination of the conventional
motifs and action with a freedom in the posture which happily
achieves the grotesque. The tradition of ivory inlays incised or
in low relief with Egyptian and Mesopotamian motifs continued into the Iron Age, being attested in pieces from Ahab's
palace at Samaria (ninth century) and from the palace of the
Assyrian kings at Nimrud (Kalhu), certain of the latter
preserving Mycenaean motifs which had been a feature of
Canaanite ivory-work in the Late Bronze Age.

Generally the Canaanite artist was more successful in his
representation of animals, as in the ivory comb from Megiddo Plate 53
at the end of the Bronze Age, where a dog pulls down an *Fig. 54*
ibex. Here the artist has given a fine impression of action and
there is a happy combination of the natural and the stylized
imposed by the panel in which the artist worked. The Megiddo
hunting scene incidentally suggests the source of inspiration,
recalling the posture of the ibex on the gold bowl from Ras Plate 6

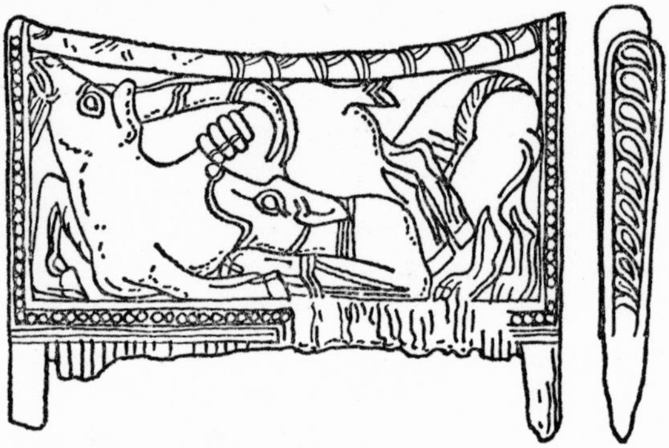

Fig. 54. Hunting scene on an ivory comb from Megiddo (after Harden)

Fig. 55 Shamra and even more the ibex on the gold-plated dagger hilt from Zapher Papoura in Crete. Indeed Mycenaean ivory-reliefs of hunting scenes and even of a suckling cow from Knossos suggest the original of the Canaanite examples. In the grip of the dog *under* the ibex there is a fine stroke of originality.

In a careful study of this subject R. D. Barnett distinguishes Egyptian, Anatolian, and Mycenaean motifs in Canaanite ivory-work, the first associated with Palestine, as in the incised scenes in ivory plaques from Megiddo (thirteenth–twelfth centuries) and Tell el-Farʿa in the Wadi Ghazzeh (thirteenth century), the second probably with north Syria, as in the relief of a lion and an ointment-pot carved with a seated sphinx, both of which suggest features of sculptures from the gateway of the Hittite capital Boghazköi. Barnett makes the feasible suggestion that this reflects the political division between the Egyptian sphere of influence in Palestine and on the Syrian coast and that of the Hittites in inland Syria. The Mycenaean motifs which we have noted raise the question of workmanship. They may reflect a third, or Mycenaean, school in one of the Mycenaean settlements in Canaan in the Late Bronze Age, such as Minet el-Beida or Tell Abu Hawam. On the other hand they may be the work of Canaanite craftsmen influenced

Fig. 55. Lion and ibex in a hunting scene on the gold bowl from Ras Shamra and on a sword hilt from Zapher Papoura, Crete (after Schaeffer and Evans)

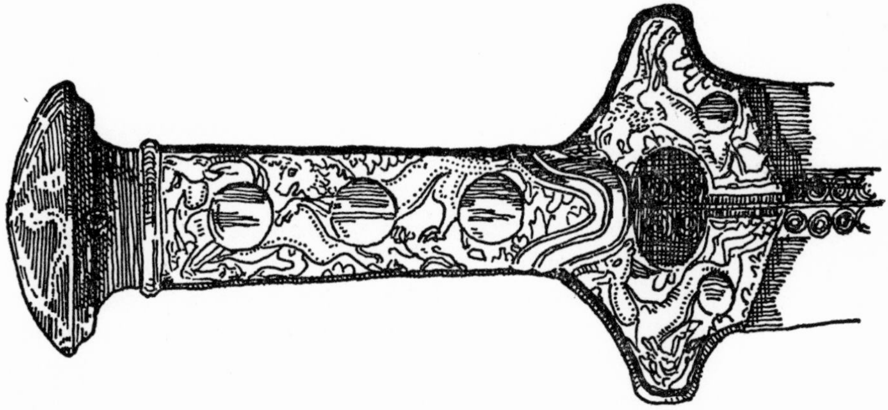

by Cretan or Mycenaean prototypes. A comparison with those relatively sophisticated Western types suggests Canaanite workmanship.

The Canaanite artists are not so successful in their reproduction of lions on a large scale in basalt. These are found in Plate 54 the sanctuary of Hazor and at the entrance to the palace of Alalakh (Atchana), where they stand as guardians in a fashion set in Upper Mesopotamia, probably by the Hurrians, and surviving till Assyrian times. The body is carved in low relief on squared basalt slabs, the tail in both cases curving up apparently from under the legs to the flank, the end tuft being represented by a circle. This mutual feature indicates a common source of inspiration. The head is done in the round, that at Hazor with the mane being much more naturalistic than those at Alalakh. The paws of the Hazor lion are naturalistic, those at Alalakh being crudely stylized. Unfortunately the badly-weathered head of the Hazor lion does not permit of an adequate impression of the degree of naturalistic representation. The attitude of another lion on an orthostat from Hazor with its forequarters upright, as distinct from the crouching position of the Alalakh lions, suggests alertness and massive power in head and shoulders. The hindquarters, however, are quite inadequate, and in those cases the artists are apparently handicapped by the hard, rough medium of the basalt. The Alalakh artist has certainly not emancipated himself from his crude Hurrian prototype, the tradition of which survives in the crude orthostats from the ninth-century Aramaean palace at Tell Halaf.

Plate 55 The double-registered relief of a fight between a lion and a dog from the temple of Mekal at Bethshan is on a much higher plane. The upper register depicts a lion and a dog rampant in combat, snarling, with muscles taut; in the lower register the dog is locked round the lion's hindquarters, into which it sinks its teeth, while the lion makes off with his tail between his legs, but otherwise apparently unperturbed. The heads in the upper register and that of the lion in the lower one are particularly good, and the whole is reminiscent of the lively animal representations in late Assyrian sculpture. Here the sculptor has overcome the difficulty of working in basalt and has emancipated himself from the heavy, lifeless tradition which he represents. The theme, feasibly taken by the late L. H. Vincent to be the expulsion of plague and death from the notorious malarial region of Bethshan with its abundant water and lush vegetation, is appropriate to the locality and might suggest the local origin of the sculpture, and indeed there is abundance of basalt immediately north of Bethshan. If this were so, the piece would be a really remarkable monument of Canaanite art. It has been claimed as north Mesopotamian, as indeed its technical affinities suggest, having been brought to Bethshan after one of the Egyptian expeditions to Mitanni in the sixteenth or fifteenth century, or perhaps done at Bethshan by some captive Mitannian artist. This is still an open question, and, if the Bethshan lion is *sui generis* in Canaan, it is also without parallel in Upper Mesopotamia at this time, as Dussaud points out in claiming it for native Canaanite art.

A notable specimen of Canaanite sculpture is the sarcophagus of King Ahiram of Byblos, which the context of two alabaster vessels of Ramses II and Cypriot pottery and Mycenaean ivory-work dates to the thirteenth century. This shows the characteristic Canaanite combination of foreign and native motifs. The king is shown bearded, seated on a high-backed throne, whose sides, as in the Megiddo ivory, are two winged sphinxes. His feet rest on the footstool, and in his right hand he holds a goblet and in his left a lotus flower drooping to symbolize death, as in Egyptian art. Before him is a table with food, conceivably just such as the ivory-fretted stand from the palace of Ras Shamra, and he is served by his retainers male and female. The end-panels are filled each with four female figures, apparently all with breasts bare, and skirts with a curious flounce, which is the conventional indication of dancing, in this case part of the mourning rite. The first two either rend or beat their breasts, and the other two either beat their heads or pour dust on them or tear their hair in grief. Here the composition is good, the details, such as the food on the table and the dresses, being reproduced as well as the coarse limestone would allow. The features of all the figures are

Plates 56, 57

conventional and lifeless, though even in spite of rigid convention the attitudes of the mourning women on the end-panels admirably convey the theme. The sculpture on the gabled lid, though of no artistic merit, is interesting. Two figures are shown in full-length effigy, one on each half; one holds a fresh lotus-flower and the other the lotus drooping. The latter is obviously the dead king. It is uncertain whether the former represents the deceased as he had been in life, his temporary revival after death, which the funeral feast may have been intended to effect, or the survival of the defunct in his successor, 'The King is dead! Long live the King!' The theme of the death of the king and the provision for his future by the funeral feast is effectively and not unpleasingly rendered, the somewhat heavy, conventional style suiting the monumental character of the work.

If the artistic initiative of the Canaanites was limited, they were familiar with *objets d'art* of foreign provenance and inspiration. Their rulers prized such pieces as the handsome battle-axes with shapely splayed blade cast in bronze in a piece with the socket, sometimes in the form of a lion's head, as in the specimen from Ras Shamra (Late Bronze Age) and sometimes with projecting spikes, as in a fine example also from Ras Shamra from the Middle Bronze level (*c.* 1900–1750), or the axe in a votive deposit of the fourteenth century at Bethshan. *Fig. 28e* This wide-splayed blade with the long supporting tang under the socket, giving the effect of a thumb and outstretched fingers, makes a very pleasing effect by the sheer boldness and grace of the double curve from spikes to blade. A plainer blade, of steel, round which the bronze socket was cast to give the impression of lions spewing forth the metal, and the forequarters of a crouching boar in place of the metal spikes at the back of the socket, has already been mentioned as possibly deriving from Mitanni in Upper Mesopotamia, being inspired probably from further east or from the Caucasus, as is sug-

Plates 42, 43

gested by even more shapely examples of the same technique from Luristan on the Iranian plateau. The fine flowing lines of the Bethshan axe suggest specimens from the Caucasus. *Fig. 29*

Syria and Palestine profited from the *pax Aegyptiaca* in the sixteenth century, especially after the rapprochement between Egypt and Mitanni from the end of the fifteenth century until the Hittite aggression in Syria under King Shubbiluliuma from *c.* 1360. In this period, when Egypt was represented by governors, district officers, and garrisons, Canaanite rulers and their families were especially open to Egyptian influence, being often educated in Egypt. The local fertility-goddess, for instance, was generally represented with the coiffure of the Egyptian Hathor, as in gold pendant reliefs from Ras Shamra and Tell el-ʿAjjul and in moulded clay plaques, and the local gods Baal and Reshef have Egyptian emblems of divinity in sculptures of this time from Ras Shamra and Bethshan. At Minet el-Beida, the seaward suburb of Ras Shamra, Egyptian prototypes were imitated with technical success. The store of a local cosmetic merchant, for instance, yielded alabaster vessels of Egyptian design but of local stone. A statuette of a bronze falcon, the bird of Horus, with a uraeus, exhibits the same influence, the bronze being inlaid with gold to pick out the plumage of the bird. The intimate attitude of affection in the ivory relief of the royal pair of Ugarit surely reflects the naturalistic freedom of Akhnaten's period, shockingly executed as the work may be. Plates 29, 30 Plates 22, 23 *Fig. 56*

From the fifteenth century until the end of the Bronze Age Mycenaean pottery is a regular feature of Canaanite sites, and we have already noted Mycenaean settlements at Ras Shamra, Minet el-Beida, and Tell Abu Hawam. The settlement of Aegean colonists, probably refugees from Crete, possibly via Cyprus, was a strong stimulus to native art, as we have already noted in our study of the ivory-work. Generally, however, as in ceramics, the Aegean prototypes suffered debasement at the

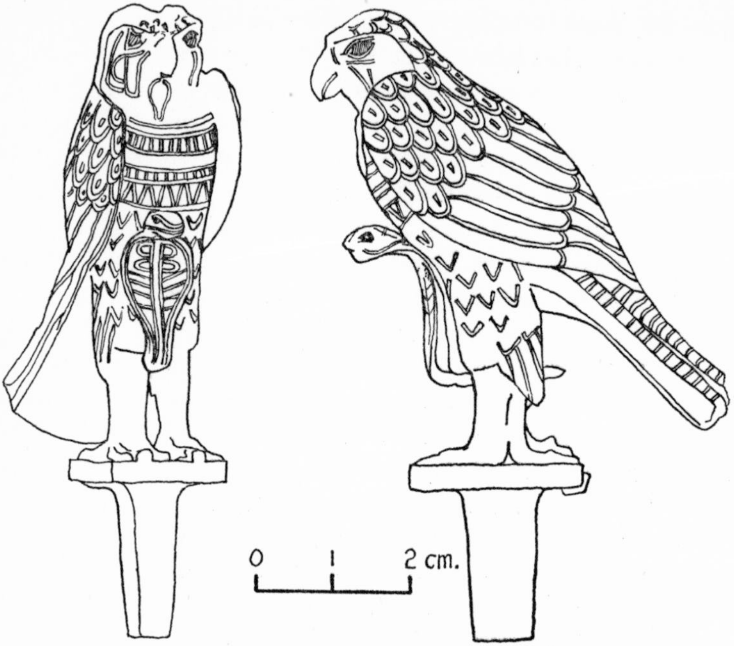

Fig. 56. Bronze falcon inlaid with gold from Minet el-Beida, fourteenth to thirteenth century (after Schaeffer)

hands of native artists. The finest specimens of Mycenaean art were probably the work of native Mycenaean craftsmen, such as the narrow graceful vases painted with an octopus, and the vase moulded with a female face and painted in various colours and finished in glaze. The expression, pleasant in spite of damage, and the arrangement of curls reflect the frescoes of the palace of Knossos. The same tradition is reflected in the fertility-goddess represented in relief on an ivory lid of a cosmetic box from Ras Shamra. The naked bust, flounced skirts, curls and pleasant expression of the figure sitting between the two caprids, to each of which she offers a plant, again suggests the frescoes of Knossos. The animals are particularly well done. Though known in this connection in Mycenaean art they

Fig. 57

Plate 32

strongly suggest the motif familiar in painted Canaanite pottery and on seals of two caprids rampant beside a fruit-tree, a theme which reaches back to Sumero-Akkadian art in tombs from the III Dynasty at Ur. The Canaanites may have introduced this theme to Mycenaean art, but the goddess is certainly the work of a Mycenaean artist.

From the same period and under the same influence a patera and bowl in gold repoussé-work from Ras Shamra make Plates 6, 7 a striking impression of the wealth and luxury of this cosmopolitan metropolis of Canaan in the Late Bronze Age. The latter with its three concentric panels bounded and divided by borders of Mycenaean spirals and such a typically Canaanite Plate 6 design as a row of pomegranates, as on a bronze tripod found in a sacred deposit at Ras Shamra, indicates conflation of Plate 31 Mycenaean and Canaanite traditions. The outer panel, depicting two short-kilted figures killing a lion, lions attacking bulls and cervids, with an Egyptian sphinx and a Mesopotamian winged bull confronting the well-known Canaanite representation of the sacred tree, or stylized palm, betrays at least two other sources. The posture of an ibex and a lion pouncing upon it, where the ibex is outlined under its profile by an apparently superfluous line of dots, is exactly reproduced in a lion pulling down an ibex on a gold-plated dagger-hilt *Fig.* 55 from Zapher Papoura in Crete, aptly cited by Professor Schaeffer. The *horror vacui* in the general composition is rather reminiscent of the debasement of Mesopotamian motifs of animals in conflict at the hands of the Anatolian Hurrians. In the second panel with its symmetrical arrangement of two lions facing opposite directions and two bulls confronting each other in the attitude of the charge, separated by a stylized tree, the predominating influence is Western in the lively and naturalistic representation of the bulls, though the stylized palm is typically Canaanite. The middle panel, about a central rosette, is relieved by the arrangement of five caprids instead of

four; two pairs of these and a single animal reach up to the stylized tree in an attitude which recalls the motif in the ivory
Plate 32 relief of the 'Lady of the Beasts'.

The patera makes a better aesthetic impression with its single theme of the chase by the bowman in a light chariot
Plate 7 with his dog pursuing an antelope, a bull, a cow and her calf, while another bull attacks the chariot from behind and the dog flies over his head as he tries to keep pace with the chariot. The flowing movement of the figures makes a complete circle

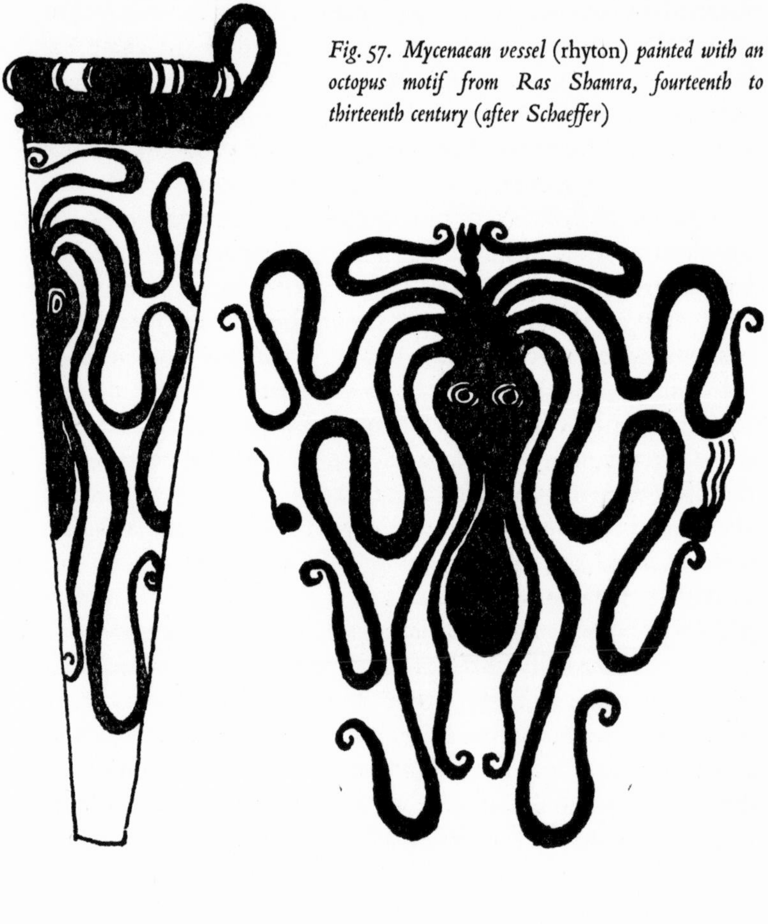

Fig. 57. Mycenaean vessel (rhyton) *painted with an octopus motif from Ras Shamra, fourteenth to thirteenth century (after Schaeffer)*

in the broad inner panel, but with these bold figures the artist remains content. In the centre are four cervids. Again the native Canaanite influence is exhibited in the features of the bowman and the light four-spoked chariot-wheel, while the natural features and the flying motion of the animals is Mycenaean, being paralleled by the flying gallop of lions in flight on the gold-inlaid dagger from Tomb IV in the citadel of Mycenae. Plate 58

It is not easy to determine whether this work is Canaanite inspired by Mycenaean art and patronage or *vice versa*. The somewhat indiscriminate mixture of styles and motifs in the bowl, however, suggests that the work, if not Canaanite, was at least 'provincial Mycenaean', as is indicated by a comparison with the bull-hunting scenes on the cups from the *tholos* tomb at Vaphio in Laconia. Plates 59–61

It used to be freely stated by a number of writers that there was no distinctive Canaanite art. This conception arose when knowledge of Canaan was limited to certain sites on the Phoenician coast, generally from the time when Hellenistic forms predominated. The excavation of earlier strata, notably from the second millennium, at the sites we have studied in both seaward and landward areas of Syria and Palestine force us to revise this opinion. The Canaanites, even if it must be admitted that they depended largely on external stimulus, were ready to attempt new forms and styles suggested by Egypt, Mesopotamia, Crete, Mycenae, or Anatolia. If they copied, they did so with a high degree of technical skill. Occasionally, if they had scope, they infused some of the native spirit into their work, but generally this was not very original. Their best work was done in ivory reliefs or in the round, where they transmitted the traditions of animal representation from Crete and Mycenae to the first millennium, when their wares were diffused to Assyria. But when all is said, native Canaanite art in plastic media had its decided limitations.

On the extant evidence the highest artistic achievement of the Canaanites was in literature. The regular rhythm of the mythological texts and their association with the cult, and indeed rubrics in a certain mythological text which culminates in the myth of the birth of the Morning- and Evening-star suggest that music was developed, and the administrative texts mention singers, probably among the temple personnel. Here again their geographical situation disposed the Canaanites to receive influences from their neighbours. An inscription on a pen-case among the Megiddo ivories mentions a female singer Kerker, or Kurkur, or Kulkul, the singer of Ptah, who had at that time apparently a temple at Askalon, and the Prince of Byblos in the time of Wenamon (*c.* 1100) had also an Egyptian female singer Ta-net-Not, but she is mentioned only in a secular capacity. Through such as Kerker, pieces like Akhnaten's Hymn to the Sun, known in its Hebrew adaptation in Psalm 104, may have been introduced to Canaan, and the short colourful love-lyrics in the Song of Solomon seem to owe something to Egyptian influence, mediated possibly through the repertoire of such as Ta-net-Not. Several hymns of praise in Akkadian syllabic cuneiform transliterated into Canaanite alphabetic cuneiform at Ras Shamra indicate the direct influence of Mesopotamian psalmody. As our citations from the Amarna Tablets indicate, however, there was also a native Canaanite tradition of psalmody, the memory of which is conserved in the Hebrew Psalter. Apart from obvious Canaanite influence in form, motif, and imagery, the 'natives' Heman and Ethan are mentioned as authors respectively of Psalms 88 and 89. They are already legendary figures together with Chalcol and Darda when the saga of Solomon's wisdom and greatness was recounted (I K. 4.31), so that there is little reason to doubt that 'native' in this case means 'Canaanite'. To be sure, the tradition in I K. 4.31 esteems them rather as sages than as poets, but in the ancient Semitic tradition wisdom and poetic skill were both manifestations of the spirit and were often combined, especially in such a serious calling as that of the temple singer. The description of these persons in I Kings 4.31 as 'the sons of Mahol' is suggestive. This does not refer to their family affinity, but means 'of the guild of choristers' or the like, as W. F. Albright first proposed.

Apart from their music, the nature and variety of which we must merely conjecture, literature, as has been said, remains the highest artistic attainment of the Canaanites. In them, as in the Hebrews, passionate involvement in the great moments of their religion evoked an acute sense of the dramatic.

Selected Bibliography

Introduction

ABEL, F. M., *Géographie de la Palestine* I, 1933; II, 1938

BALY, D., *The Geography of the Bible*, 1957

DUSSAUD, R., *Topographie Historique de la Syrie Antique et Mediévale*, 1927

SMITH, G. A., *A Historical Geography of the Holy Land*, 26th ed., 1935

Habitat and History

ALDRED, C., *The Egyptians*, 1961

BREASTED, J. H., *A History of Egypt*, 1906

DUMONT, A., Indo-Iranian Names from Mitanni, Nuzi, and Syrian Documents, *Journal of the American Oriental Society* LXVII, 1947, pp. 251–253

Appendix to R. T. O'Callaghan, *Aram Naharaim*, 1948, pp. 149–155

HARDEN, D. B., *The Phoenicians*, 1962

KNUDTZON, J. A., *Die el-Amarna Tafeln*, 1907–14.

NOTH, M., Die syrisch-palästinische Bevölkerung des zweiten Jahrtausend vor Chr. im Lichte neuer Quellen, *Zeitschrift des Deutschen Palästina-Vereins* LXV, 1942, pp. 9–67

OLMSTEAD, A. T., *A History of Palestine and Syria*, 1931

POSENER, G., *Princes et Pays d'Asie et de Nubie. Textes Hiératiques sur des Figurines d'Envoûtement du Moyen Empire*, 1940

SCHAEFFER, C. F. A., *Ugaritica* I, 1939; II, 1949; III, 1956; IV, 1963

Stratigraphie Comparée et Chronologie d'Asie Occidentale, 1948

SETHE, K., *Die Ächtung feindlicher Fürsten, Völker und Dinge auf altägyptischen Tongefässscherben des Mittleren Reiches,* Abhandlungen der preussischen Akademie der Wissenchaft, Phil. hist. Klasse, 1926

VAUX, R. DE, Études sur les Hurrites, *Vivre et Penser*, 1941, pp. 194–211

WEIDNER, E. F., *Boghazköi Studien. Politische Dokumente aus Kleinasien* I, 1923

WILSON, J. A., *The Burden of Egypt*, 1951
WOOLLEY, SIR L., *A Forgotten Kingdom*, 1953

Daily Life

ALBRIGHT, W. F., The Excavation of Tell Beit Mirsim, II, The Bronze Age, *Annual of the American Schools of Oriental Research* XVII, 1938
BARROIS, A. G., *Manuel d'Archéologie Biblique* I, 1939; II, 1953
INGHOLT, H., *Rapport préliminaire sur sept campagnes de fouilles à Hama en Syrie*, 1940
KENYON, K. M., *Digging up Jericho*, 1957
Archaeology in the Holy Land, 1960
LOUD, G., *Megiddo II*, 1948
The Megiddo Ivories, Oriental Institute of Chicago Publication 52, 1939
MACALISTER, R. A. S., *The Excavation of Gezer*, 3 vols., 1912
MESNIL DU BUISSON, COMTE DU, Fouilles à Mishrifé, *Syria* VIII, 1927; X, 1929; XI, 1930
Le Site archéologique de Mishrifé-Qatna, 1935
MONTET, P., *Byblos et l'Égypte*, 2 vols., 1928
PETRIE, SIR W. F., *Ancient Gaza* I–IV, 1931–4
Beth Pelet I and II, 1930 and 1932
Gerar, 1928
ROWE, A., *The Topography and History of Bethshan*, 1930
The Four Canaanite Temples of Bethshan, 1940
SCHAEFFER, C. F. A., *Ugaritica* I, 1939
The Cuneiform Texts of Ras Shamra-Ugarit, 1939
TUFNELL, O., HARDING, G. L., and INGE, C. H., *Lachish* II, 1940
VINCENT, L. H., *Canaan d'après l'exploration récente*, 1907
YADIN, Y., *et al., Hazor* I, 1958; II, 1960

Society

BOYER, G., and NOUGAYROL, J., *Mission de Ras Shamra* VI; *Le Palais Royal d'Ugarit* III. *Textes accadiens et hourrites des Archives est, ouest et centrales*, ed. C. F. A. Schaeffer, 1955
GRAY, J., *The Legacy of Canaan*, chapter V, 1957
VAN SELMS, A., *Marriage and Family Life in Ugaritic Literature*, 1954

VAUX, R. DE, *Ancient Israel: Its Life and Institutions*, 1961
VIROLLEAUD, C., Les villes et les corporations du royaume d'Ugarit, *Syria* XXI, 1940, pp. 123–151
Lettres et documents administratifs de Ras Shamra, *Syria* XXI, 1940, pp. 247–276
Textes administratifs de Ras Shamra, *Revue d'Assyriologie et d'Archéologie Orientale* XXXVII, 1940, pp. 11–44
Nouveau textes administratifs de Ras Shamra, *Revue d'Assyriologie et d'Archéologie Orientale* XXXVII, 1940, pp. 129–153
Le Palais Royal d'Ugarit II; *Textes en Cunéiformes alphabétiques des archives est, ouest, et centrales*, ed. C. F. A. Schaeffer, 1957
WISEMAN, D. J., *The Alalakh Tablets*, 1953

Religion

ALBRIGHT, W. F., *The Archaeology of Palestine and the Bible*, 3rd ed. 1935
From the Stone Age to Christianity, 1940
Archaeology and the Religion of Israel, 3rd ed., 1953
BAUER, H., Die Gottheiten von Ras Shamra, *Zeitschrift für die Alttestamentliche Wissenschaft* N. F. X. 1933, pp. 81–101; XII, 1935, pp. 54–59
BAUMGARTNER, W., Ras Shamra und das Alte Testament, *Theologische Rundschau* XII, 1940, pp. 163–188; XII, 1941, pp. 1–20, 85–102, 157–183
Ugaritische Probleme und ihre Tragweite für das Alte Testament, *Theologische Zeitschrift* III, 1947, pp. 81–100
BEA, A., Archaeologisches und Religionsgeschichtliches aus Ugarit-Ras Schamra, *Biblica* XX, 1939, pp. 436–453
COOK, S. A., *The Religion of Ancient Palestine in the Light of Archaeology*, 1930
CUMONT, F., Adonies et Canicule, *Syria* XVI, 1935, pp. 46–49
DHORME, E., Le dieu parent et le dieu maître, *Revue de l'Histoire des Religions* CV, 1932, pp. 229–244
DUSSAUD, R., *Les découvertes de Ras Shamra (Ugarit) et l'Ancien Testament*, 2nd ed., 1941
Les Origines canaanéens du sacrifice israëlite, 2nd ed., 1941
La religion des Phéniciens, 1945

EISSFELDT, O., Ras Shamra und Sanchuniathon, *Beiträge zur Religionsgeschichte des Altertums*, Heft 4, 1939
El im Ugaritischen Pantheon, *Berichte über die Verhandlungen der sächsischen Akademie der Wissenschaften zu Leipzig*, Phil. hist. Klasse, Band 98, Heft 4, 1941
GRAY, J., *The Legacy of Canaan*, 1957, chapters II and IV
HOOKE, S. H., *The Origins of Early Semitic Ritual*, 1938
HVIDBERG, F. F., *Grad og Latter i det Gamle Testament. En Studie over Kanaanäisk-israelitisk Religion*, 1938; English translation and revision, 1962
KAPELRUD, A. S., Jahves tronstigningsfest og funnene i Ras Sjamra, *Norsk Teologisk Tidsskrift*, 1940, pp. 38 ff.
Baal in the Ras Shamra Texts, 1952
MOWINCKEL, S., Das Thronbesteigungsfest Jahwehs und der Ursprung der Eschatologie, *Psalmenstudien* II, 1922
POPE, M., *El in the Ugaritic Texts*, Supplements to *Vetus Testamentum*, vol. II, 1955
SCHMIDT, W., Königtum Gottes in Ugarit und Israel, *Beiheft zur Zeitschrift für die alttestamentliche Wissenschaft* 80, 1961

Letters and Literature

DHORME, E., Un nouvel alphabet sémitique, *La Revue Biblique* XXXIX, 1930, pp. 571–577
Le déchiffrement des textes de Ras Shamra, *Journal of the Palestine Oriental Society* XI, 1931, pp. 1–6
DIRINGER, D., *The Alphabet*, 1948
Writing, 1962, chapters V and VI
DRIVER, G. R., *Semitic Writing*, 1948
Canaanite Myths and Legends, 1956
DUNAND, M., *Byblia Grammata*, 1945
DUSSAUD, R., *Les découvertes de Ras Shamra (Ugarit) et l'Ancient Testament*, 2nd ed., 1941
EISSFELDT, O., Mythus und Sage in den Ras Schamra Texten, *Arabistik, Semitistik, und Islamswissenschaft*, 1944, pp. 263–283
GARDINER, A. H., and PEET, T. E., *The Inscriptions of Sinai*, 1919
GASTER, T. H., *Thespis*, 1950

The Canaanites

GINSBERG, H. L., Ugaritic Myths, Epics, and Legends, *Ancient Near Eastern Texts relating to the Old Testament*, ed. J. B. Pritchard, 1950

GORDON, C. H., *Ugaritic Literature*, 1949

Ugaritic Manual, 1955

GRAY, J., The Krt Text in the Literature of Ras Shamra, *Documenta et Monumenta Orientis Antiqui*, vol. V, 1955

The Legacy of Canaan, 1957

Texts from Ras Shamra, *Documents from Old Testament Times*, ed. D. W. Thomas, 1958

HARRIS, Z. S., *A Grammar of the Phoenician Language*, American Oriental Series, 8, 1936

LANGHE, R. DE, *Les Textes de Ras Shamra et leurs Rapports avec le Milieu Biblique de l'Ancien Testament*, 1945

Myth, Ritual, and Kingship in the Ras Shamra Tablets, in *Myth, Ritual, and Kingship*, ed. S. H. Hooke, 1958

PATTON, J. H., *Canaanite Parallels to the Book of Psalms*, 1944

PEDERSEN, J., Die KRT Legende, *Berytus* VI, 1941, pp. 63–105

VAUX, R. DE, Les Textes de Ras Shamra et l'Ancien Testament, *La Revue Biblique* XLVI, 1937, pp. 526–555

VIROLLEAUD, C., *La Légende phénicienne de Danel*, 1936

La Légende de Kéret, Roi des Sidoniens, 1936

La légende du roi Kéret d'après de nouveaux documents, *Mélanges syriens offerts à M. René Dussaud*, 1939, pp. 755–762

Légendes de Babylone et de Canaan, 1949

Articles on the Baal myth and other texts in *Syria* XII, 1931 ff.

Art

BARNETT, R. D., Phoenician Ivory Carving, *Palestine Exploration Fund Quarterly Statement*, 1939, pp. 4–19

CONTENAU, G., *La Civilization Phénicienne*, 1949, pp. 120–139

DUSSAUD, R., *L'Art Phénicienne du IIme Millenaire*, 1949

KANTOR, H., The Aegean and the Orient in the Second Millennium BC, *American Journal of Archaeology* II, 1947, pp. 86–89

LLOYD, S., *The Art of the Ancient Near East*, 1961

LOUD, G., *Megiddo Ivories*, Oriental Institute of Chicago Publications, 52, 1939

MARINATOS, S., *Crete and Mycenae*, 1960

PARKER, B., Cylinder Seals from Palestine, *Iraq* IX, 1949, pp. 1–42

PRITCHARD, J. B., *Palestinian Figurines in relation to Certain Goddesses known through Literature*, American Oriental Society Publications, 24, 1943

SCHAEFFER, C. F. A., *Ugaritica* I, 1939

Also official reports of excavations cited in bibliography to *Daily Life*

Sources of Illustrations

I should like to thank and also acknowledge the help that I have received from the following persons and institutions in supplying plates used in this book: L'Ecole Biblique et Archéologique Française, 45; Professor Yigael Yadin, The James de Rothschild Expedition at Hazor, 26, 27, 47, 54; The Director of the Palestine Archaeological Museum, Jerusalem, 5, 21, 40; The Wellcome Trust, 3; The Director of Antiquities of the Syrian Arab Republic, Aleppo, 6, 7, 29, 42, 43, 53; and Damascus, 8, 9, 10; The Oriental Institute, The University of Chicago, 11, 12, 14, 15, 16, 18, 19, 24; The British School of Archaeology in Egypt, 38; Dr K. M. Kenyon, The British School of Archaeology in Jerusalem, 33, 34, 35, 37; The Director of the National Museum of Antiquities of the Republic of Lebanon, Beirut, 1, 4, 39, 44, 46, 56, 57; Musees Royaux d'Art et d'Histoire, Département égyptien, Brussels, 2; Staatliche Museen zu Berlin, 17; The Trustees, the British Museum, 20; The University Museum, Pennsylvania, 23, 55; The Louvre Museum, 22, 28, 31, 46, 49, 50; Thames & Hudson Archives, 12, 13, 25, 30, 32, 46, 48, 51, 52, 58, 59, 60, 61.

The three maps, figures 1, 2, and 3, were drawn by Mr H. A. Shelley of Cambridge; figures 5, 7, 9, 10, 16, 17, 20, 25, 30–34, 36, 39, 41, 42, 50 and 56 were drawn by Mr Michael L. Rowe of Cambridge, and figures 8, 12, 21, and 27 were drawn by Mr Michael Spink of Thames & Hudson. Figures 15, 18, 46–48, 51, and 54 are from Thames & Hudson archives. All other figures are the work of Mr James Somerville, A.R.I.B.A.

THE PLATES

2

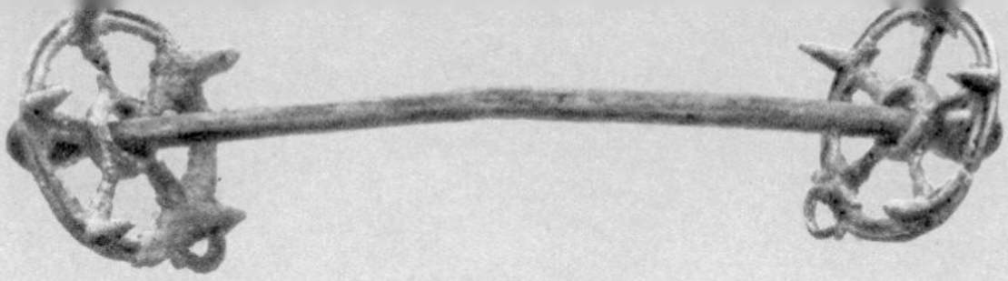

5

6

7

8

9

10

11

12

13

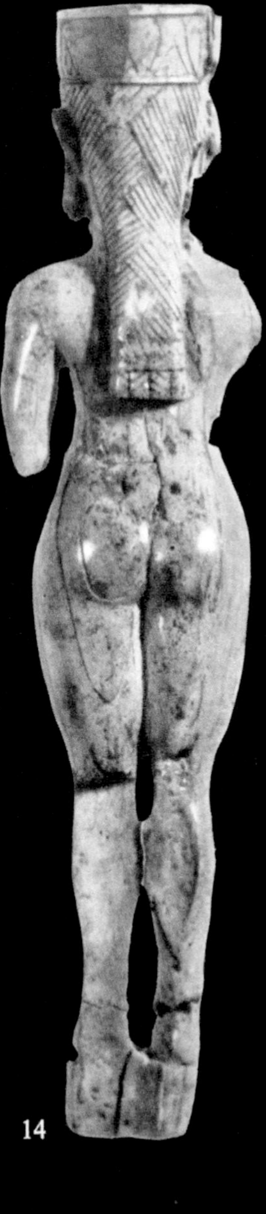

14

15

16

17

19

20

21

22

23

24

25

26

27

28

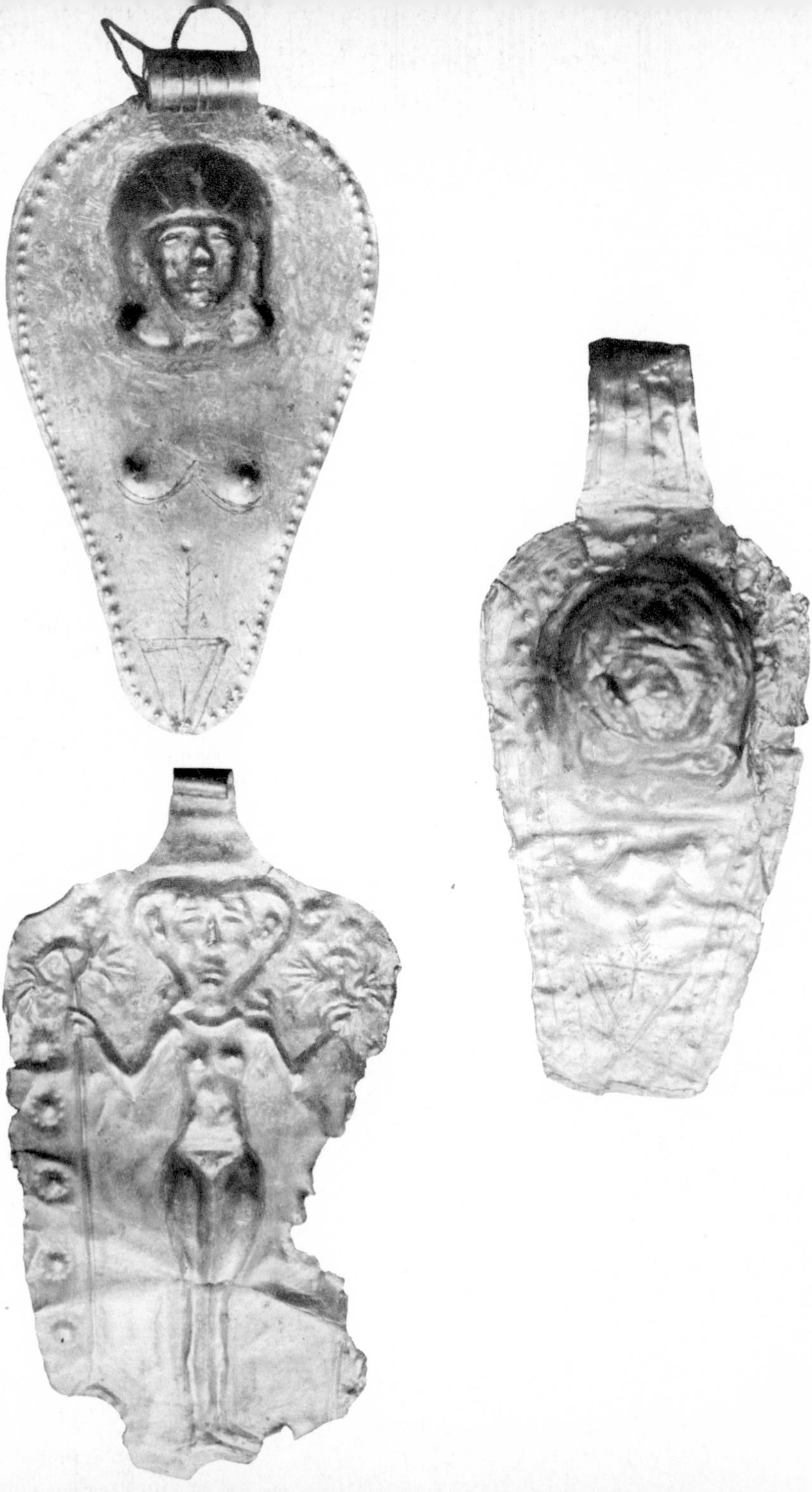

29

30

31

32

33

34

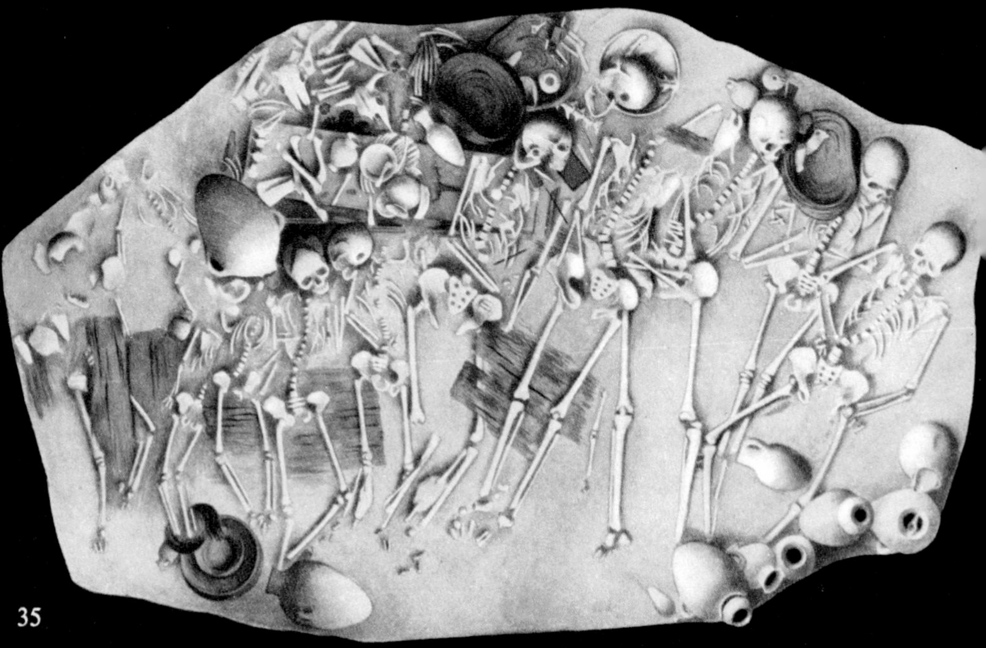

35

36

37

38

39

40

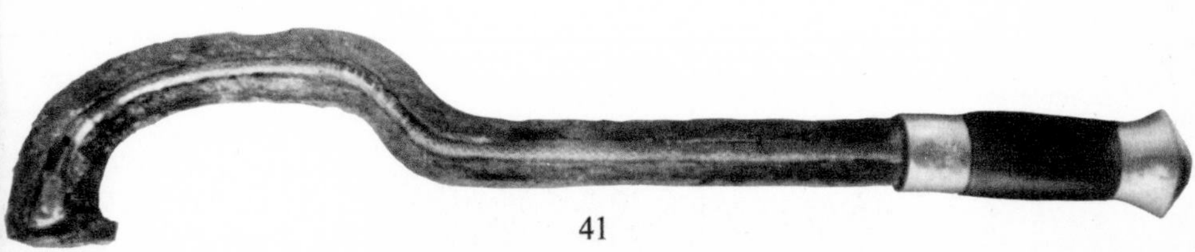

41

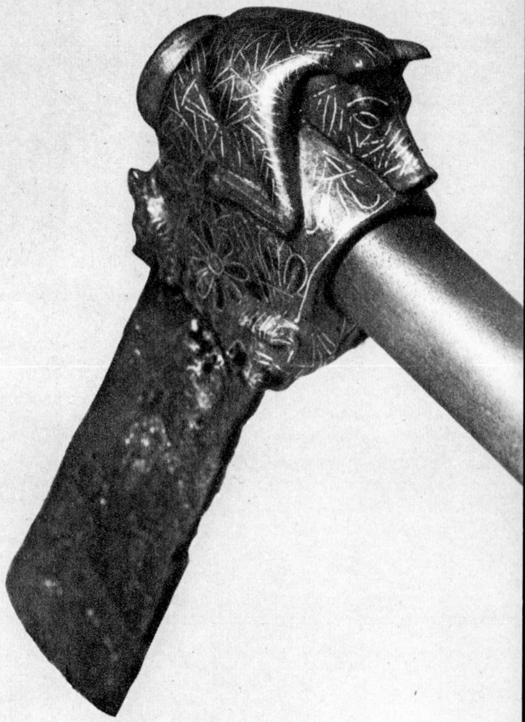

42

43

44

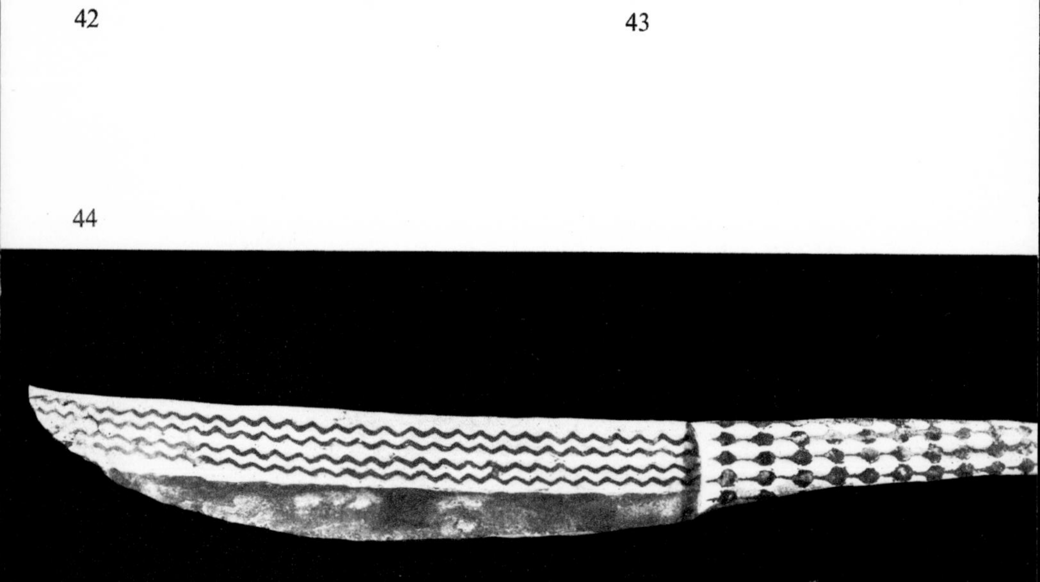

45

46

47

48

49

50

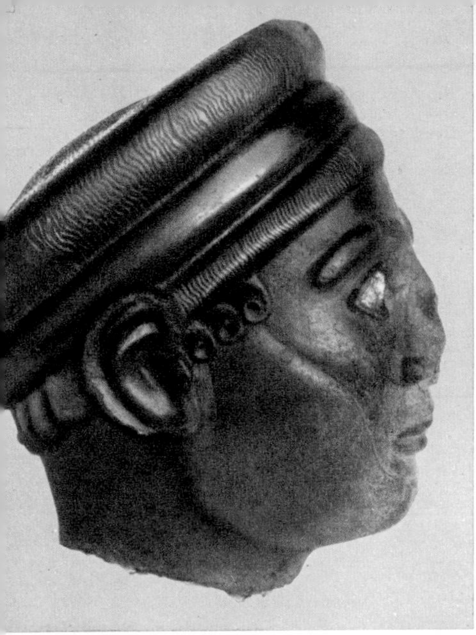

51

52

53

54

55

56

57

58

59

60

61

Notes on the Plates

1 Gold diadem from the royal tombs of Byblos (nineteenth–eighteenth centuries). In the centre is the *djed*-pillar symbolizing the renewal of kingship in Egypt, flanked by *was*-sceptres, the Egyptian symbol of well-being, and *ankh* signs symbolizing life, surmounted by the hooded cobra (uraeus) denoting Egyptian royalty. Many of the objects in precious metal from the royal tombs of Byblos are gifts from the Pharaoh to the rulers of this important Syrian seaport, and others are of native workmanship reproducing Egyptian originals.

2 Execration figurine with hieratic inscription naming chiefs of localities hostile to the Pharaoh, who were ritually destroyed by the magical use of such figurines. Possibly they represented prisoners of war, whose morale was thus broken and who were then state slaves. The figurine is one of a number recovered from a Cairo antique dealer and identified by G. Posener with similar figurines in the Museum of Antiquities in Cairo. He traced them by reports and photographs to a late nineteenth-century level in the excavations at Saqqara, which the palaeography of the texts supports.

3 The Hyksos glacis (*c.* 1730–1580) of earth faced with limestone chips and plaster at the north-west corner of Tell ed-Duweir (Lachish). The angle of the slope is 29° and it was surmounted by a wall. Formerly supposed to have been designed to keep the enemy beyond the range of his weapons but within the range of the composite bow of the defenders, which is associated with the Hyksos, the glacis is now thought to have been a protection against the battering-ram.

4 Silver fluted vessel of Cretan provenance from the tomb of King Abu Shemi at Byblos, nineteenth century.

5 Bronze bit from the Hyksos period at Tell el-ʿAjjul, spiked to facilitate rapid manœuvring in chariot warfare, introduced to Canaan in the eighteenth century.

6 Gold bowl in repoussé work with hunting scenes on the outer panel, having Mycenaean features in the movement of the animals. The border at the outer edge and between the first and second panels is engraved with a Mycenaean spiral design. The latter border on its inner side is decorated with the typically Canaanite design of pendant pomegranates. In the middle, the Canaanite motif of the stylized tree divides the figures of lions and bulls, and the third panel around the central rosette is decorated with another Canaanite design of caprids reaching up to the 'Tree of Life', here stylized in the middle panel. This is an excellent illustration of the mixture of artistic influences in Canaan in the period *c.* 1450–1365, and the piece may be either Canaanite under Mycenaean influence or, more probably, provincial Mycenaean. From Ras Shamra. *See* C. F. A. Schaeffer, *Ugaritica* II, 1949, pl. 1.

7 Gold patera with a hunting scene in which a bearded Semitic figure in a two-horse chariot pursues a wild bull, a cow and calf, and a caprid, while another wild bull charges the rear of the chariot. The dog appears to be tossed by the charging bull. The flying gallop of the animals indicates Mycenaean influence. The flowing movement in the outer panel contrasts with the unimaginative motif of five caprids about a central circle in the inner panel. From Ras Shamra, *c.* 1450–1365. *See* C. F. A. Schaeffer, *Ugaritica* II, 1949.

8 Small ivory head from the palace of Ras Shamra in the Late Bronze Age. Professor Schaeffer now considers this piece to be a portrait sculpture of a queen and not a king of Ugarit. The features, on the other hand, may be fashioned after those of Baal in bronze figurines from Ras Shamra and Minet el-Beida (fig. 22). *See* C. F. A. Schaeffer, *Ugaritica* IV, 1963, p.25, figs. 24, 26.

9 Ivory panel from the royal bed in the palace of Ras Shamra in the Late Bronze Age. This, the inside, presents intimate scenes from the life of the royal family. In the first panel on the right the queen prays to the fertility-goddess in the third panel to the left. In the second panel from the right the king and queen caress, the queen's abdomen being discreetly emphasized to suggest pregnancy. In the third panel from the right twin youths

suck the breasts of the fertility-goddess with Hathor coiffure surmounted by the horns of divinity and an astral disc. The two figures probably represent one, the heir, who is described in the *Krt* text from Ras Shamra as suckled by fertility-goddesses. The figure may be represented twice for the sake of symmetry. The two panels on the left may exhibit the king as a hunter in his youth before marriage. In association with the fertility theme of the whole we should emphasize the motif of the stylized Tree of Life at each end. Ivory itself may have been prized for its magical properties to promote potency as at present in unsophisticated societies in the East. *See* C. F. A. Schaeffer, *Syria* XXXI, 1954, pp. 1–2, pl. VII.

10 Outer side of the ivory panel from the royal bed in the palace of Ugarit. The fertility theme is continued with the supplication of the queen in the first panel on the right to the nude fertility-goddess (in the first panel on the left) with the lotus plant and *ankh* sign, both Egyptian symbols of life. The king slays a lion in the second panel from the left and dispatches an enemy in the third panel from the left. *See* C. F. A. Schaeffer, *Syria* XXXI, 1954, pp. 1–2, pl. VII.

11 Ivory plaque from the palace of Megiddo, *c.* 1350–1150, with Hittite figures and emblems in relief. This piece may support R. D. Barnett's thesis that Canaanite craftsmen in ivory worked for a clientèle familiar with Egyptian, Mycenaean, and Hittite culture in the north of Syria.

12 Ivory plaque for inlay with griffin in low relief, from the palace of Megiddo, *c.* 1350–1150. The main features and attitude of the figure reproduce those of the murals of the griffins in the throne-room of the palace of Knossos (*cf.* plate 13).

13 Murals of griffins from the throne-room of the Minoan palace at Knossos, Crete, destroyed *c.* 1400.

14 Fragmentary ivory figurine, the front of which is entirely damaged, from the palace of Megiddo, *c.* 1350–1150.

15 A Canaanite maiden. Fragmentary openwork plaque carved on both

sides, with tenons for insetting into furniture. The pupils of the eyes are inset with glass paste.

16 Openwork ivory plaque of Bes, the benevolent dwarf of Egyptian religion, the protective genie of pregnant women, children at play, and people asleep. He carries stylized life-symbols (*ankh*), and the tree which projects behind him may be the Tree of Life. His tongue is grotesquely prolonged. The posture is cunningly contrived to fit the limited framework of the panel in such a way as to increase the impression of the grotesque. The plaque is tenoned at top and bottom for insetting into furniture. From the palace of Megiddo, *c.* 1350–1150.

17 Letter from Abdi-Khipa, King of Jerusalem, to the Pharaoh, either Amenhotep III, 1411–1375, or Amenhotep IV (Akhnaten), 1375–1358, in Akkadian syllabic cuneiform, the diplomatic medium of the period throughout the Near East, from el-Amarna.

18 Foreign prisoners of Ramses III (1168–1137) depicting racial types known in Canaan, from right to left, Amorite, Philistine, Hittite, and Bedouin. The first figure on the left is a Libyan. From the temple of Ramses III at Medinet Habu.

19 Egyptian sculptured and inscribed stele (*c.* 1550–1100) of Reshef, the Canaanite god who slew men in mass by war or plague. He is one of the Canaanite gods worshipped in Egypt in the Late Bronze Age, and introduced as a result of the Egyptian campaigns in Canaan after the expulsion of the Hyksos (*c.* 1580), probably by the great number of Canaanites settled in Egypt as prisoners of war, hostages, or mercenaries. The figure wields a fenestrated axe and carries a spear and shield, which may identify him with a small bronze figurine from Megiddo. The gazelle-horns on the front of his helmet identify him in the opinion of the writer with the god Mekal on the stele from Bethshan (Fig. 8), whose name, we think, means 'Annihilator' (Hebrew *mekalleh*).

20 The Canaanite fertility-goddess in an Egyptian sculpture of the Late Bronze Age, named Qodshu, i.e. possibly 'the sacred prostitute' *par excellence,* Canaanite Ashera, the mother-goddess, or, more probably,

Astarte, as indicated by her cult-animal the lion. Her fertility propensities are indicated by her nudity, the fresh lotus flower which she holds (the Egyptian symbol of life), and the two serpents in her left hand, which, annually sloughing their skin, symbolize the power of renewal of life. On her right stands the ithyphallic Egyptian fertility-god Min, whose fertilizing properties are indicated by his phallus and by the erect vegetation behind him. On her left stands Reshef denoted by his gazelle-symbol on his Semitic headdress. His warlike character is indicated by the spear in his right hand, whilst in his left he carries the *ankh*, or Egyptian life-symbol. His association with the fertility-goddess and Min well emphasizes the dual character of Reshef as the god of life or death. Such a god might well be worshipped in a malarial region such as Bethshan, where he is depicted as Mekal (Fig. 8).

21 Stele with inscription of Seti I from Bethshan, *c.* 1313, mentioning 'Apiriw of the mountain of Yarmuth', probably just north of Bethshan.

22 The stele of Mami 'the royal scribe and keeper of the house of silver'. It was dedicated to 'Seth of Sapuna', i.e. the Canaanite Baal, whose seat *par excellence* was Mount Saphon (*Khursag Khasi*, the Mount Casius of the Greek geographers) on the north horizon of Ras Shamra.

23 Stele from Bethshan dedicated by Hesi-Nekht, an Egyptian official, to 'Antit, Lady of Heaven and Mistress of all the gods', who is invoked 'for the life, strength, and health of the *ka* (soul) of Hesi-Nekht', thirteenth or twelfth century. The goddess wears the Egyptian double crown and, clad in a long robe, carries the *ankh* and the *was*-sceptre, the Egyptian symbols of life and of well-being. The stele is now in the Palestine Archaeological Museum, Jerusalem, Jordan.

24 A Canaanite fortress attacked by Ramses III with native spearmen manning the crenellated battlements, towers, and probably an independent redoubt within the wall and adjacent to it. Note the corbelled projection of the battlements, which gave the defenders the same advantages practically as later machicolation. From the temple of Ramses III at Medinet Habu.

25 Standing-stones in the 'Obelisk Temple' at Byblos (eighteenth century), possibly memorials of theophanies (*cf.* Jacob's pillar at Bethel, Genesis 35.14–15).

26 Alignment of pillars (Hebrew, *masseboth*) with a seated divine image in black basalt in the Late Bronze Age sanctuary (Area C, I A) at Hazor. The crescent to which the hands are raised on one of the pillars and the inverted crescent on the breast of the figure suggest a lunar cult. The hands indicate perhaps the intercessory function of a notable ancestor of the community remembered as one who especially possessed the divine favour (*beraka*) and as such a fitting intercessor. It was probably the association of ancestors with the local places of worship, the so-called 'high places' of the Old Testament, that made them so popular in ancient Israel. The horizontal slab in front of the pillars is thought to be a table for offerings.

27 Late Bronze Age shrine at Hazor, tripartite, with entrances on the same axis, as in Solomon's Temple.

28 Stele of the Canaanite Baal, Hadad, with the lightning-spear striding above either mountains, clouds, or the waters of the earth and sky. C. F. A. Schaeffer, the excavator, dates it to the first half of the second millennium BC at Ras Shamra.

29 Natural and stylized gold pendant reliefs of the Canaanite fertility-goddess. Note the Egyptian features of the Hathor coiffure, and the lotus plants, the symbol of life. From the Late Bronze Age at Ras Shamra. *See* C. F. A. Schaeffer, *Syria* XIII, 1932, pl. IX.

30 Moulded clay plaques of the Canaanite fertility goddess(es), commonly found in Bronze Age strata at sites throughout Palestine and Syria. They were probably domestic amulets to promote childbirth, possibly acquired after the vows at a shrine, *cf.* I Sam. 1.10 ff.

31 Bronze stand, probably for a laving-bowl, from Ras Shamra, fifteenth or fourteenth century BC. The rim is decorated with pendant pome-

granates, as were the tops of the pillars Yachin and Boaz in Solomon's Temple. Height 12 cm.

32 Mycenaean ivory relief of the fertility-goddess and the beasts, two caprids, to which she offers plants. The figure of the goddess with bare breasts, her hair style, flounced skirt, and pleasant facial expression derives from Crete, but the motif of the two rampant caprids feeding on the plants suggests a Mycenaean variation of the native Canaanite theme of the two caprids rampant feeding on the Tree of Life. In view of the sacred tree, natural or stylized, symbolizing the mother-goddess Ashera, and in fact called the Ashera, the goddess in the place of the Tree of Life is highly significant. The piece is the lid of an unguent-box from Minet el-Beida by Ras Shamra from the fourteenth century.

33 Single male burial with a bronze dagger in a small, neatly-hewn rock-chamber at the foot of a vertical shaft. This is one of several different forms of burial *c.* 2000, which coincided with an intermediate period in the occupation of Jericho. The site was then occupied by squatters, associated with Amorite tribesmen, possibly those who disrupted the sedentary civilization of Palestine and Lower Egypt towards the end of the third millennium. The diverse types of burial at the same period at Jericho, as in the plate, and at Tell el-ʿAjjul, Megiddo, and Gibeon suggest the co-existence of independent tribal groups, which the names of several chiefs in the same locality in the Egyptian Execration Texts (*c.* 1850) also indicate.

34 Disarticulated burial at Jericho in the intermediate period when the site was occupied by squatters, probably Amorite tribesmen, *c.* 2000. The disarticulated remains are thought by the excavator, Miss K. M. Kenyon, to indicate that the body had been brought some distance by nomads to a tribal burial ground.

35 Family tomb at Jericho of the Hyksos period (*c.* 1600), preserving much of the furniture of daily life in a well-to-do family of the end of the Middle Bronze Age. Note the pottery, which is typical of the period. The burials were simultaneous, the result probably of a local epidemic,

and the fact that the tomb was not thereafter re-opened is thought to have been the cause of the excellent state of preservation of the perishable fibres owing to the gases of the decomposition of the bodies having been undisturbed by the outer air.

36 Wall painting from the tomb of Khnum-hotep, at Beni Hasan, Upper Egypt, *c.* 1890, depicting Absha 'the ruler of a foreign land' (*hyk khwsht*, 'Hyksos') bringing a company of 37 Asiatics with antimony as eye-cosmetic to Egypt. The variety of patterns in the clothing, the bellows on the asses and the harp and weapons, especially the composite bow, indicate craftsmen, and the throwing-stick and captive gazelle and ibex indicate competent desert hunters. The group has a modern analogy in the tinker clans of Nawar and Suleyb, who travel the desert marches with asses, and this group may be itinerant smiths, such as the Biblical Qenites.

37 The interior of the house of a well-to-do Canaanite family of the Hyksos period reconstructed from contemporary tomb remains at Jericho.

38 Gold work from the Late Bronze Age (sixteenth–twelfth centuries) at Tell el-'Ajjul at the mouth of Wadi Ghazzeh.

39 Gold pectoral from the royal tombs of Byblos (nineteenth or eighteenth century) in the form of a falcon, the bird of Horus, the fertility-god, who was thought to be incarnate in the living Pharaoh. In Egyptian royal pectorals the falcon holds in his claws the seal of the Pharaoh. Here the claws hold merely the finials of a decorative band, which may indicate either a native imitation, or, if the piece is a gift from the Pharaoh to the King of Byblos, an adaptation with respect to the subordinate status of the foreign ruler.

40 Figures of flies and a louse (?) in solid gold from the Late Bronze Age at Tell el-'Ajjul. These may have had a prophylactic value against disease (*cf.* the gold mice in I Sam. 6.4) or have been Egyptian merit awards, 'the gold of valour' mentioned by the Pharaohs.

41 Bronze parade scimitar with the Egyptian uraeus (royal hooded cobra)

and the name of King Ypshemu'abi inlaid in gold. From the tomb of Ypshemu'abi at Byblos, eighteenth century.

42 Socketed axe with finely tempered iron blade set in bronze cast in the form of lions spewing forth the blade. The socket is damascened in gold to pick out features on the heads and the open flowers, which are a feature of Hurrian white-painted pottery from Upper Mesopotamia *c.* 1600. The axe is considered by the excavator, Professor Schaeffer, to be of Mitannian origin. From Ras Shamra, *c.* 1600. *See* C. F. A. Schaeffer, *Ugaritica* I, 1939, pl. XXII.

43 The back of the socketed axe in Plate 42 cast in the form of the fore-quarters of a crouching boar, with hair and features damascened in gold. The boar is a quite un-Semitic motif, but was used without inhibition among the Hurrians, as at Nuzu near Kirkuk, where it was used on wall-plaques.

44 A decorative knife from the royal graves of Byblos (nineteenth century) with a blade of silver damascened in gold, the handle patterned in gold foil and black niello-work.

45 A pottery kiln from the end of the third millennium (Early Bronze Age) at Tell el-Farʿa by Nablus (probably Biblical Tirzah).

46 Bronze dagger with incised signs from a tomb at Tell ed-Duweir (Lachish) of the Hyksos period, *c.* 1700–1600. The signs probably mark an early stage in the evolution of the alphabet, but except the head, which all agree represents *r*, they are of uncertain significance, and no probable reading has been proposed.

47 Inscribed liver tablet for instruction in augury from the Late Bronze Age at Hazor. This is the first inscribed liver tablet to be found in Palestine, though others have been found without inscriptions. Since the publication of the Hazor example some have been found in an important deposit of the Late Bronze Age at Ras Shamra.

48 Sculpture of the weather-god Teshub from the King's Gate of the Hittite

capital at Boghazköi (Hattušaš), the costume and attitude of which recalls that of Baal with the lightning-spear from Ras Shamra (plate 28) and other figurines from Syria and Palestine. The socketed axe with five projecting spikes at the back of the socket recalls the bronze socketed axe from the Late Bronze Age at Bethshan (Fig. 28*e*).

49 Figurine of a seated goddess from Ras Shamra, once inlaid with gold, and dated to the period 1900–1600 BC by the excavator, who emphasizes the Armenoid features. If this reflects the background of the artist the goddess is probably Khipa. Height 24·8 cm.

50 Standing figurine of a god from Ras Shamra of bronze inlaid with electrum. Schaeffer gives a date of 1900–1600 BC. The head-dress suggests Anatolian affinities. Height 20 cm.

51 Life-size stone head of a king of Alalakh, probably Yarim-lim (eighteenth century) from Atchana. This has been feasibly taken as the work of a North-Syrian school of art perpetuating the ancient Sumerian tradition mediated to the region in the ascendancy of the III Dynasty of Ur (*c.* 1940 BC), which seems to be supported by the affinity of the work with such pieces as the sculpture of Gudaea of Lagash.

52 Sumerian sculpture of praying ruler, probably Gudaea, from Telloh (ancient Lagash) of the twenty-second century.

53 Bronze weights in the form of recumbent animals from Ras Shamra, fourteenth century.

54 Lion orthostat in basalt from a Late Bronze Age sanctuary at Hazor.

55 Panel of lion and dog in black basalt from the Mekal temple (fourteenth century) at Bethshan. The lion is known as the cult-animal of Reshef, whom we identify with Mekal ('the Annihilator'), and this panel in his temple may reflect his dual character of giver of life and death, *cf.* Fig. 8. On the provenance and artistic affinities see text p. 174. Now in the Palestine Archaeological Museum, Jerusalem.

56 Stone sarcophagus of King Ahiram of Byblos with reliefs of funeral rites for the dead king who is seated in the underworld, as indicated by the drooping lotus in his hand. A feast is spread before him, perhaps as the last rites in the funeral ceremonies, as a passage in the Baal-myth of Ras Shamra indicates. The panel is supported by couchant lions and bounded by a rope-design surmounted by lotus buds and flowers, indicative of Egyptian influence. On the lid is an inscription, which W. F. Albright would date on palaeographic grounds to the eleventh century. The archaeological context of two alabaster vessels of Ramses II, Cypriot pottery, and Mycenaean ivory-work, however, suggests a date in the thirteenth century.

57 The end-panel of the sarcophagus of King Ahiram of Byblos depicts females whose flounced skirts are the conventional rendering of a dance, here a mourning rite, in which they loose their upper garments and dishevel their hair. Two lacerate their breasts, which we know from the Baal-myth of Ras Shamra to have been a mourning rite, and the other two tear their hair or put dust upon it (*cf.* the hands on the head as a mourning rite in Jeremiah 2.37).

58 Dagger blade of bronze inlaid with a design in gold, silver, and black niello illustrating the flying gallop of animals; it shows interesting affinities with scenes depicted on the patera of Plate 7. From Shaft Grave IV in the citadel of Mycenae.

59 Gold repoussé work depicting a wild bull attacking his hunters on a drinking-cup from Vaphio in Laconia *c.* 1500. The naturalistic vigour of this and the scenes in the next two plates demonstrates by contrast the provincial character of the hunting scenes of Mycenaean inspiration in Canaanite art, as in Plates 6 and 7.

60 Wild bull caught in a net in gold repoussé work on a cup from Vaphio.

61 Catching a wild bull by means of a decoy cow in gold repoussé work on the second cup from Vaphio.

Index